SOLID GOLD SUCCESS STRATEGIES FOR YOUR BUSINESS

Don Taylor

American Management Association

New York • Atlanta • Chicago • Kansas City • San Fransico • Washington, D.C.

Brussels • Mexico City • Tokyo • Toronto

This publication is designed to provide accurate and authoritative
information in regard to the subject matter covered. It is sold with the
understanding that the publisher is not engaged in rendering legal,
accounting, or other professional service. If legal advice or other expert
assistance is required, the services of a competent professional person
should be sought.

Library of Congress Cataloging-in-Publication Data

Taylor, Don (Donald D.)
     Solid gold success strategies for your business / Don Taylor.
          p.   cm.
     Includes bibliographical references and index.
     ISBN 0-8144-7914-6
     1. Success in business.   2. Strategic planning.   I. Title.
HF5386.T3188   1996
658.4'012—dc20   96-475
                                                                            CIP

Printing number

10   9   8   7   6   5   4   3   2   1

To **Christi Lyn**:

When you were born, your mother and I cried. Our tears were tears of joy and pride. We still feel the same joy and pride each time we think of you. May God bless and guide your every step until you walk on streets of gold.

Contents

Acknowledgements

I risk committing great sins of omission by trying to name those who played a vital role in this book. Nonetheless, a few deserve recognition.

Therefore, a special "thank you" goes to Ann Stanford and Shane Smith. To Ann for her tireless hours of typing, reformatting, and editing. And to Shane who provided motivation, organizational wisdom, and encouragement.

Also deserving of special kudos are Charlie McMahon and Dorsey Wilmarth. It was their casual conversation in 1989 that launched my newspaper writing career. Thanks, men, for the confidence and encouragement.

Thanks also to all of my editors and publishers who have faithfully carried every "Minding Your Own Business" column. And to my readers, who hold my feet to the fire, make suggestions as needed, and offer praise when appropriate.

I am grateful to Mary Glenn and the competent crew at AMACOM for their continuing faith and support. Once again they prove that you can make a silk purse from a sow's ear.

And to my bride of twenty-five years, Sue, who has never doubted, always encouraged, and who has endured every deadline. "Honey, I'm home."

Part One

Business Builders

I have a theory about how to prosper in business. I believe that success in any venture is the long-term result of doing simple things well. The difference between keeping your customers and closing your doors is *not* having a name that ends in M-A-R-T. It is taking care of the details day after day, with your goal being continuing improvement. The business owner who is obsessed with improvement will get better, stronger, faster, tougher, smarter, *and*—if he or she stays with it long enough—wealthy.

The first six chapters of this book are devoted to ideas, concepts, stories, facts, and theory that will help you grow and become prosperous in business. Whether you're a long-time veteran, a brand-new start-up, or a wanna-be, you will benefit from these pages

During the past eight years, I've worked one on one as a consultant with more than 1,500 businessmen and women. Prior to that, I spent nearly ten years as a retailer and another ten years in corporate marketing and advertising in Chicago and Los Angeles.

The ideas I share here are more others' than my own. Personal lessons can be expensive and painful. You can save a lot by learning from the experience of others.

If you decide to invest in this book, you will benefit in two ways. Part One will help you grow your business. Part Two will help you grow personally. Both are important to your health, wealth, and happiness.

Chapter 1

Marketing: The Midas Touch

According to Greek legend, King Midas was granted the power to turn everything he touched into gold. If you want to grow your business or enrich your personal career, marketing can be your "Midas touch."

Marketing is the art of creating, satisfying, and keeping customers, and building relationships that can make your career skyrocket. A thorough understanding of marketing principles will help you increase your business's sales and profits. Even if you work for someone else, you can use the fundamentals of the marketing mix to increase your value to your employer and climb the corporate ladder.

Whether you're a small-business owner struggling to compete with the megastores or an aspiring employee who wants to earn more and increase your worth, marketing can be your golden opportunity. However, you shouldn't take my word for it— experience it for yourself.

This chapter contains golden nuggets of truth that have been gleaned from the best marketing mines. Use it to learn how to build and nurture business relationships, create effective advertising, conduct low-cost market research, understand and adjust the key elements of your marketing mix, improve your selling skills, and get free publicity for your company.

The Ten Commandments of Advertising

If Moses had been sent up the mountain by the local business community, he might have come down with a different set of tablets. Under his arm he might have carried the Ten Commandments of Advertising.

Most owners and managers of small businesses struggle with the question of how to promote their business successfully. Many of them feel that they waste about half of their advertising budget. The problem is figuring out which half.

With that in mind, I submit to you the following thoughts on advertising:

I. *Thou shalt plan ahead.* Too often we wait to make decisions about advertising until a media salesperson comes calling. Spur-of-the-moment judgments are usually not effective. The first step in improving your advertising effectiveness is to create a plan for the year. You should budget a specific amount for promotion, whether it is a set amount or a percentage of sales.

II. *Thou shalt not consider advertising as an expense.* Yes, I know that that is how advertising shows up on your income statement. However, if you consider advertising as a cost of doing business, you may be tempted to trim the amount you spend on it or cut it out altogether. Please refer to Commandment III.

III. *Thou shalt regard advertising as an investment.* Promotion costs are not an expense, they are an investment in future business. Just as a farmer plants seed to ensure a harvest, a business must advertise to grow a new crop of customers.

IV. *Seek ye first the customer's interests, needs, and wants.* A big advertising budget won't guarantee increased sales of unneeded or unwanted items. Create every advertisement with your target customer's needs in mind instead of promoting what you want to sell.

V. *Thou shalt stress the benefits.* Your advertisements should point out the advantages to the customer of doing business with you. Don't sell stuff; sell benefits. For example, don't sell a car;

sell style, fuel economy, and dependability. Don't sell a book; sell hours of pleasurable entertainment and profitable knowledge. Make it easy for your customer to see your benefits.

VI. *Thou shalt not commit adundancy.* OK, I admit it; I made up a word. *Adundancy* is advertising redundancy— boring, repetitive, unexciting ads that run again and again. Adundancy is dull, repetitious, uninspiring ads that are used over and over and over . . . well, I guess you get the picture.

VII. *Thou shalt be unique.* Dare to be different. Don't be afraid to try something uncommon. Keep everything simple and consistent with your image, but make your ads out of the ordinary. When you travel, always be on the lookout for creative ideas that you can adapt for your use.

VIII. *Thou shalt make use of thy co-op budget.* If you don't know about co-op advertising, contact your media representative immediately. Let your representative show you how to double the effectiveness of your advertising budget.

IX. *Thou shalt use thy media representatives.* There is a wealth of advertising knowledge available through the staffs of your local advertising media. Visit with them and explain your needs and concerns. (One note of caution: Snake oil salespeople exist in every industry.) Take time to develop a relationship of trust. If a salesperson approaches you with a "now or never" deal, choose never.

X. *Thou shalt measure thy results.* With a little planning, you can identify where your advertising dollars are producing the most results. Vary the offers and measure results. Use coupons and incentives to track responses. Above all, ask new customers how they found out about your business. Keep a record, and over time you will increase your effectiveness.

The Dying Art of Marketing

Often in workshops and seminars I ask business owners to define the term *marketing*. One of the most common answers I get is "selling." Selling is certainly a very important part of marketing, but it is only one part.

To define marketing as selling is a little like describing an automobile as an engine. Yes, automobiles have engines, but there is much more. An engine alone does not make an automobile. However, the engine does provide the "go power" for that automobile.

I believe personal selling provides the "go power" in a marketing program. Selling is a function that is critical to every business and career. Many feel that selling is also a dying art.

We All Sell

There is an old saying that nothing happens until somebody sells something. I have seen this proved again and again.

In the early 1970s, I traveled extensively in the state of Michigan. I worked in many of the cities where automobiles rolled off the assembly lines. I can still recall seeing thousands of acres of brand new cars in towns like Flint, Pontiac, Saginaw, Bay City, and Detroit. The cars weren't selling , and this caused other business to fail as well.

I can still remember the boarded-up windows of many businesses in those cities. The message is clear to me now: It doesn't matter what you can produce, your business (and others who depend on your success) will struggle if you can't sell it. This is true for big corporations, small business, and individuals.

Robert Louis Stevenson said, "Everyone lives by selling something," and he was right. A teacher lives by selling ideas and sound educational principles. A business consultant lives by selling solutions to difficult problems. An automobile dealer lives by selling dependable transportation and status. A welder lives by selling mechanical skills.

Some of you are thinking, "Wait a minute, Don, what about the 'dying art' statement. If everyone is selling something, how can selling be a dying art?"

The perceived value of selling is declining because few workers today realize how important it is to their livelihood. Most do not understand that their only job security comes from a healthy economy, in which businesses are selling their products and services at a profit. Even if you work for the government, taxes on business profits and wages paid by those businesses generate the salary you receive.

Some Thoughts on Selling

Despite the common misconception, no one is a born salesperson. You must develop sales skills in the same manner you develop other skills—through knowledge and practice.

In my more than forty years of selling experience—for the record, I started trying to sell my mother on the concept that cookies were good for me when I was four years old—I've learned a few good selling basics that I'd like to share with you.

1. Always tell the truth.
2. Sell the benefits, not the features.
3. Selling is a service—a service with value.
4. Don't underestimate the value of product knowledge; it is important.
5. Don't argue with a potential customer; you may win the argument, but you'll lose the sale.
6. Put yourself in your customers' shoes—even if they don't fit.
7. Look for "I'm ready to buy" signals, then ask for the business.
8. Don't laugh at your competitors' selling errors; there is a lesson to learn if you're alert.

9. The sale isn't over when you get the money; give follow-up service and sell the customer again.
10. Don't bet the farm on customer loyalty; you're only
    as good as your last sale.
11. Don't wait until you're in trouble to start selling; dig
    the well before you're thirsty.

The Marketing Mix

One of my small-business clients once told me, "I'm not
sure what marketing is, but whatever it is, I don't think we're
doing it very well." This client expressed the feelings of a
great many business owners who struggle with marketing
their products or services.

Marketing is a proactive strategy that enables you to
pounce on every business opportunity. I define *marketing* as
the art of creating, caring for, and keeping customers. The
marketing process starts when you focus your efforts on identifying the needs of your customers. Once you analyze the
need and target the selected customer, you must have the
right marketing mix to guarantee customer satisfaction.

The marketing mix is a little like a jigsaw puzzle. When you
put the correct puzzle pieces in just the right places, they all fit
together and form the picture of success. The marketing mix
puzzle has six main pieces: product, price, place, positioning,
people, and promotion (I often call them marketing's six Ps).

Marketing's Six Ps

Each element of the marketing mix plays an important
role in your potential business success. If you get just the right
mix, you win big. If you get one element wrong, you lose.

Wal-Mart is an excellent example of a business that has
the correct marketing mix. The company is successful because
it offers the products that most Americans buy regularly. In

the eyes of its customers, its prices offer real value. Wal-Mart's stores are in highly visible, easy-to-access locations, and its promotions are effective.

In business there is a saying that "the best never rest." This is true in Wal-Mart's case. The company constantly makes changes in the mix. It introduces new products. It creates in-store promotions to test both pricing and promotion strategies. New stores are opened in carefully selected locations all around the country.

Adjusting the Mix

Let's assume for a moment that your business is not as successful as Wal-Mart. Perhaps you even feel that the mass merchandisers and the category killers are about to do you in. If that is the case, it's time to adjust your mix.

Start with your *product*. Does it offer real benefits to your customers? Is your product or service unique? Do you offer visible quality and value? You can improve this element of your mix by focusing your efforts on providing added value for your customers. Look for new products and services that meet needs and satisfy wants.

Next, look at your *pricing*. Remember that your pricing level must be fair to both you and your customer. If your prices are too low, you won't cover all expenses and earn a profit. If they are too high, customers will cease to perceive value and will seek other places to buy. Improve your purchasing practices and use a variable pricing strategy to gain on the competition.

Next, take a look at the *place* element of the marketing mix. Is your location convenient to your customers? Does your facility make a good first impression? Are you open when your customers want to do business with you? (If not, adjust your hours to please your customers.) If you take your product or service to your customers, is your place of business centrally located in your distribution area?

The next marketing factor is *positioning*. Your market position is based on the advantages and benefits you give your customers. Make a list of the specific benefits you offer that no one else can match. The longer the list, the stronger your position. If you can't think of any advantages your customers gain by doing business with you, don't expect your customers to be loyal to you.

Another critical element in your mix is *people*. To serve customers quickly and effectively, friendly, courteous, knowledgeable people are required. I often see businesses stumble in this area. They have good products, fair prices, and strategic advantages, but they lose the customer by having the wrong people on the front line.

Finally, consider how you *promote* your business. Promotion includes advertising, but it's more than that. Handing out business cards and introducing yourself with a ten-second commercial are also good promotion strategies.

Good promotion will help you establish a positive business image. You can put your best foot forward by emphasizing your strengths and the benefits you offer your customers.

Good marketing is creating, caring for, and keeping customers. With some adjustment you can make marketing's six Ps work for you.

What Do You Know?

Asking "What do you know?" or, more appropriately, "What do we know?" is an inexpensive form of market research. Good research will generate useful information. All businesses need information if they are to compete effectively. In this, the information age, it is critical that we periodically assess what we know.

In every business, there are several areas about which you should gather information. For example, if you are a typical business owner, you would benefit from gathering information on your customers and suppliers, industry trends, and competitors. All of this information is market research in its most simple form.

Customer Research

Learning more about your customers is a healthy first step for every business. Customers are the only reason your business exists. Therefore, it is reasonable to assume that the more you know about your customers, the better you can serve them.

For example, you might begin with *demographic character-istics*. These are simple ways of dividing customers into classes or segments. Typical characteristics include age, marital status, income level, gender, race, geographic location, and household size.

You can also look at psychographic and behavioral characteristics. *Psychographic characteristics* are measures of attitudes, interests, opinions, and feelings. Knowing them will help you understand what your customers want, what they feel strongly about, and how they see your business. You can use *behavioral characteristics* to describe and define why customers behave the way they do when shopping. You can use this information to learn how your customers compare prices, select stores, choose products, and arrive at purchasing decisions.

Using the Information

Research information can help you position your business to serve customers more effectively. When combined with personal observation and contact, it can prove very profitable.

For example, the owner of an upscale dress shop that targeted wealthy, mature women noticed that her older, retired customers often brought their husbands along when shopping. The men soon grew tired of waiting and began to fidget and fuss. The wives would frequently leave without purchasing anything or quickly purchase something and often return it later.

The owner took quick steps to remedy the problem. She had a contractor build a small cubicle, and she equipped it with three comfortable chairs and a small color television. She located it near the dressing area and next to the full-length mirrors.

She encouraged the husbands to sit and enjoy the news or a ball game while their wives shopped. As a result, sales went up and returns went down. Both husbands and wives were more content with the shopping experience.

The manager of a children's clothing store noticed a similar situation with restless children. To solve the problem, she turned a portion of her store into a children's play area. She carefully decorated the area with colorful cartoon characters and provided toys and games.

Because she knew her customers well, she selected only toys and games that were both educational and fun. The mothers, who could relax now that the children were both content and learning, spent more time shopping. As a result, sales per customer increased nearly 11 percent the following year.

Identifying a position or niche should be a goal of every business. Your niche is the environment or areas where you can serve your target customers better than anyone else can. To create a position of lasting value, you must have something unique to offer your customers

To begin, you must identify and understand your customers' unfulfilled needs. Then you can move to fill them. If you cannot see any unmet need, or if you can't identify any benefits, you may not have a niche or position to fill. To survive in a "no-niche" environment, you must take business away from others. Usually, this means head-to-head price-driven competition.

Ten Good Questions

Before you try to position or reposition your business, you should ask some questions. Here are ten good "what do we know?" queries.

1. Who are your customers? How can you describe them? Can you divide them into groups or classes?
2. How much do you know about them? Do you know where they live, their lifestyles, their buying habits, and their personal tastes?
3. Do you know your customer batting average? You can calculate it by dividing the number of customers who make purchases from you by the total number of customers who come into your business.
4. Do you know what your customers think about your business? If you don't know, ask them. I think customers are flattered when business owners ask for their opinions. Finding out how your customers feel about your business can be very enlightening.
5. What do your customers think about your competition? How can you find out? Once again, all you have to do is ask them.
6. Do you know who your ten best customers are? How about the top twenty five? The top one hundred? Use your records to find out. You're not keeping customer records? Hm-m-mm.
7. Have you personally had contact with your top ten or twenty customers in the past month? In the past three months? If the answer is no, contact them today—tomorrow at the latest.
8. Do you make it easy for your customers to complain to you? According to research, 96 percent of all customers who leave a business in an unhappy state of mind never tell anyone in the business. Your task is to make it easy for customers to complain—not by providing lousy products and terrible service, but by making them feel comfortable about bringing a complaint to you. You can't solve problems that you don't know exist.
9. Do you have a follow-up program for ex-customers? If not, start one now. Find out why they are ex-customers. You may be able to overcome past difficulties and regain business.

10. Do you know what is going on within your industry? Industry trends and activity are important. Get involved with trade associations and subscribe to publications to stay informed.

Sometime soon you may be hailed with a "what do you know?" greeting. I hope you will think to yourself, "We know a lot, but we're still learning." You see, good research is a never-ending process.

A Good Sign

If you are a typical small-business owner, you probably feel that it would be nice to have more help. Would you like to hire a sales associate who would work hard for several days for a dollar or less?

Would you be interested in a worker who doesn't demand a benefits package, won't call in sick, doesn't ask for vacation during your busy season, and will accept abrupt termination without recourse or hurt feelings? The worker I'm speaking of is a good sign.

Signs can help you increase sales. Research indicates that in some cases, point-of-purchase sales increase by as much as 24 percent when a good sign is added. The research also shows that signs pointing out product benefits will generate even more sales.

Good signs will help your customers reach a buying decision. They will help your customers select the correct model, the right size, or specific features they desire in a product. Signs also help customers compare prices and give you the advantage of being able to explain hidden benefits.

Signs are also a good way to drive your megastore competitors crazy. You can change prices in minutes by putting up a new sign, whereas many discounters' prices are tied to regional or national promotions.

Good signs help you build your customers' perception of value. Professional signs add to your quality image, whereas handwritten signs look cheap.

You can use a computer, word processor, or custom sign-making machine to make your own signs in-house. There are also many businesses that specialize in quick, custom-made signs.

Here are several tips for creating good signs:

Sign Tips

- Be specific in the wording you use. Say STEEL LEAF RAKES—FLEXIBLE TINES—$4.99, not RAKES—$4.99.

- Make pricing and quantities easy to understand. LARGE PAPER CLIPS —50 FOR 49¢, not just CLIPS—49¢. Point out value: LESS THAN 1¢ EACH.

- Sell the sizzle. Why is this product unique? Identify the special benefits, such as LOCALLY GROWN or MADE IN TEXAS, then add them to your signs.

- Give your customers plain, simple facts, not hype. If you claim that your product is "improved," "fresher," or "better," prove your claims with facts.

- Use signs to explain what isn't obvious: KEYLESS DOOR LOCK—JUST ENTER YOUR 3-DIGIT CODE TO UNLOCK YOUR DOOR.

- Help the customers find the best value with the features they want. Specify additional features as the price goes up. For example, on "good, better, best," models, list two, four, and six features, respectively.

- Offer additional items. If you're selling paint, suggest brushes, masking tape, a drop cloth, and razor blades.

- Don't waste space by pointing out the obvious. Don't say ASSORTED COLORS if you can see the assortment.

- Keep your signs positive and friendly. Don't use *don't*. Say THANK YOU FOR NOT SMOKING, not DON'T SMOKE. Say SHIRT AND SHOES REQUIRED BY STATE LAW, not NO SHIRT, NO SHOES, NO SERVICE.

- Listen to customers' questions. If several customers ask the same question, you may need a sign.

• Listen to your customers' praise. When customers say, "We really like . . . because . . .," the "because" is a benefit that you should add to your signs.

• Use a sign to reinforce your advertising. Say AS ADVERTISED. If something is important enough to advertise, it deserves a sign. We know one merchant who watches his competitors' ads and matches the price with an AS ADVERTISED sign. He doesn't say who advertised it.

Move your business image up a notch with good signs. Signs are a low-cost way to increase sales and serve your customers more effectively.

It Pays to Advertise

I built a better mouse trap.
It was a sight to see.
Because it was so clever,
I knew the world would come to me.

My trap had bells and whistles
and benefits galore,
so I waited with anticipation
for the world to find my door.

But the path was never beaten,
the buyers never came.
They knew not about my mouse trap
and they'd never heard my name.

They knew not of its cleverness,
its benefits and price.
Nor of the iron-clad guarantee
to rid their house of mice.

You must take your better mouse trap,
to markets grand and glowing,

with fireworks and fanfare
and many trumpets blowing.

For no one will buy your mouse trap
unless they know about it.
You must advertise and merchandise
and then you'd better shout it.

Do not rest upon your laurels
is what I would advise,
if you want to sell some mouse traps,
it pays to advertise.

I know Whitman and Frost have nothing to worry about. Though I was tempted to emulate Charles Osgood and write this entire segment as a poem, better judgment won out.

However, I hope the poem got your attention and made this point: Promotion is important. Whether you are selling a better mousetrap or the same old widget as last year, you have to let the whole world know.

Effective advertising should both be believable and point out real benefits. You should follow proven guidelines to increase your advertising effectiveness. Here are a few that work.

Advertising Tips

• Use a simple, uncluttered layout. A print advertisement should include a lot of white space. Limit the number of items in any ad to increase the visual impact. Simple ads with photographs or artwork are more appealing than straight copy. According to research, photographs are 26 percent more effective than artwork at increasing recall. A common error is to overcrowd an ad with too many items. Stick with one dominant element to attract attention.

• Use a "grabber" headline. Studies show that 80 percent of those reading ads never go beyond the headline. Therefore, your headline must draw your reader into the body of the ad. It must deliver a benefit or promise a reward for wading through the rest of the copy. Make the most of your headline; it is the only chance you get to snag a reader.

• Deliver the goods in your copy. Effective copy will expand on the headline and point out specific benefits. Don't mention the price without pointing out the savings and value. Remember that the readers of your ad don't buy products for the sake of the product, they buy for the benefits they will receive. Pointing out the benefits will help your readers understand what's in your offer for them.

• Ask for action. An effective ad will inspire the reader to take action. As in all selling, it pays to ask for the order. Make it easy for your customers to respond. Every ad should include the name, address, and phone number of your business. Use your logo in every ad, and remember to include the hours you are open for business.

Look out, Charlie Osgood,
You clever poetic pro,
Others can rhyme, all the time,
And now the readers know.

Relationship Marketing

I'd like to offer an exciting and perhaps new concept for all small businesses. What if we started focusing on how we can best satisfy customer needs instead of just selling our products and services? What if we became obsessed with taking such good care of our customers that they become our personal friends? What if we worked so hard to satisfy our customers that they wouldn't dare stop doing business with us?

Many business owners are using this strategy to win customers' loyalty and increase sales. I believe these two results—customer loyalty and increased sales—go hand in hand.

I know some of you are thinking, "What is customer loyalty? We used to have it, but it doesn't exist anymore!" Although some experts suggest that customer loyalty is gone forever, I disagree. Many small businesses are growing and prospering by taking good care of their customers. Every day, rain or shine, they continue to build long-lasting associations with their customers. They are practicing relationship marketing.

Taking Customers for Granted

One of the reasons customer loyalty diminished in the first place may have been that businesses started taking their customers for granted. The level of care started to slip as the companies began to focus on internal needs, assuming that the customer would always be there. However, as in any other personal relationship, when you start to assume, you're in trouble.

I often hear business owners and managers argue that customers should stand by them. They tell me that they support their communities and believe that their customers should support them.

However, their customers see it from a different perspective. They may feel that better selections, cleaner floors, newer styles, and lower prices await them elsewhere. They know the business is not giving them the personal service it once did. To the customers, it is a personal issue, not a community issue.

A New England bookstore owner told me that he had once met a regular customer at a community meeting and chided him in a friendly way for not coming into the store as frequently as he had in the past. The customer responded seriously that he had been in the bookstore several times recently, but had not seen the owner there at all. He suggested that he—the customer—was spending more time in the bookstore than the owner was. The owner then realized that he needed to spend more time working the sales floor, meeting and greeting customers, and building stronger relationships.

Here are five tips for building lasting relationships with customers:

Building Relationships

1. Remember that all business is personal. People like to do business with people. In fact, most folks won't do business with companies where there is little personal contact.

2. Know your customers and stay in touch with them. Talk to them and listen to what they have to say. It is difficult to establish a relationship with someone you don't know much about. The more you know about your customers, the better you can serve them.

3. Do whatever it takes to satisfy the customer. Doing little things that customers like strengthens relationships. Even if you don't like to do something, do it if it pleases the customer. Satisfied customers tell others. Just ask any Lexus owner.

4. Promise a pound, deliver a ton. Go beyond what the customer expects. Exceed expectations. Deliver more than you promised.

5. Stay focused on providing value. No one chooses the lowest-price item every time. We all make decisions based on value, not just cost. Add value to your products and save your customers' time. You'll see sales soar.

Relationship marketing is a one-to-one strategy. It will help you win customers for life.

Free Promotion

There are two good ways to get your name in front of the public: Pay for advertising or make news. Advertising will require spending money; making news will require an investment of your time. Making news is a good business-building strategy, and many companies that have more time than money use this technique to increase their visibility.

Here's how it works. Newspapers, radio, and television all occasionally have slow news days. With a little practice, you can sow some seeds that may blossom into a flowery news story on one of those slow days.

A good way to plant those seeds is to use a written press release. Press releases can be powerful tools, and there is no real magic to preparing one.

There are two main elements to consider as you construct a good news release. The first is the content, and the second is the way you organize your information. The content is the newsworthy message that you believe the media will find interesting. The structure or organization should follow basic guidelines for press releases. Most good public relations and advertising books will describe the basic format.

Here are several proven tips for making news. Follow these suggestions to improve your company's image and visibility.

How to Make News

• Make certain that anything you send to the news media is newsworthy. For example, sidewalk sales, year-end clearances, and inventory reduction blowouts are not news. Expanding your business, winning a customer service award, or being named Dealer of the Year is news.

• Be creative. We've seen some pretty ordinary happenings make the front page or the six o'clock news because of an unusually creative approach.

• Start with the five W's: who, what, where, when, and why. Take the time to write down the details before you organize them into a finished press release.

• Begin with the most important information. Even on a slow news day, you'll need to get your reader's attention right away.

- Type the release on your letterhead. Double-space the text to make it easy to read.

- Keep your release short and to the point. Give your name and phone number so that you can be reached for further information. Since not all media persons work eight to five, you may benefit from giving an "after hours" or "weekend" phone number. Your goal is to make it easy for someone to get additional details.

- Your release should focus on one thought, event, or element. If you try to cover too much ground, you may make it difficult for the media person to visualize a story.

- Send your press release to the person most likely to be interested (usually the business editor or news director).

- When the newspaper picks up your press release and runs a nice story, don't let the publicity end there. Make copies and distribute them to current and potential customers. Frame a copy and place it in a prominent location in your business.

- Say thank you. News folks are like the rest of us. Thanks for a job well done is always appreciated.

If you don't feel that you are up to writing your own press releases, contact a professional. Many small public relations firms and advertising agencies specialize in this area. They may be able to provide just what you need for a very reasonable fee.

The Three Rs of Advertising

According to advertising consultant Stewart Britt, "doing business without advertising is like winking at a girl in the dark. You know what you are doing, but nobody else does." I agree wholeheartedly with Britt and would take his analogy a few steps farther. Some businesses wink with their backs turned—they don't aim the message toward the customer. Some businesses wink when the customer is looking the other way—their timing is off. Some businesses wink and get a favorable response but don't know what to do next—they didn't plan ahead.

All businesses—large or small, home-based or at the mall, cash-rich or up against the wall—can benefit from good advertising. Advertising, when properly targeted and timed, is a good investment in future business.

Many small-business owners confuse advertising awareness with advertising expertise. They see a style they like and try to use the same technique to promote their business. Frequently, this method is not effective.

You can increase the effectiveness of your ads by understanding the three Rs of effective advertising. The three Rs are getting the *right message* to the *right audience* at the *right time*. However, that's not as simple as it sounds.

The Right Audience

Let's begin with the second R, the right audience. The first question to ask is, "Who do you want to reach with your ads?" Your advertising should target your most likely customers. The better you can define your customers, the easier it is to execute the other two Rs.

Recently, I asked participants in an advertising workshop to rate potential customers for an upscale ladies' dress shop. I asked if a sixty-year-old confirmed bachelor with no female friends or relatives would be a likely customer for the store. Most of the participants shook their heads negatively or murmured no. Then one bright person in the back said, "It all depends on how he likes to dress at home." It was good for a laugh and helped drive home the point. Not everyone is a good target.

You can target potential customers by sex, age, income level, lifestyle, ethnic origin, type of business, or geographic location. Once you can identify your most likely customers, move on to creating the right message.

The Right Message

Recently, we studied more than 350 advertisements in fourteen local, regional, and national newspapers. We found that 36 percent of them touted big savings, huge sales, and tremendous discounts. Some offered up to 50 percent off the regular prices. To me, these ads imply that the merchants' prices are too high, so they are cutting prices temporarily to see if I'll buy at a lower price. Is that what you want to tell your customer?

The right message should give your customers valid reasons for doing business with you at your regular prices and markups. It should extol the benefits of your products and services. The right message will point out your good value, convenience, variety, and ability to solve problems.

The Right Time

Even if you get the right message to the right audience, you may still fail if the timing is off. Let's assume that you sell Daygo snow tires (Daygo in snow, Daygo in slush, and Daygo lots and lots of miles). If you buy a full-page newspaper ad in July, you may waste much of the message. By the time the snow flies, your value, quality, store name, and location may be forgotten.

The right time is when your customers have a need. It may also be when they have the money. Many small businesses have increased their advertising success by timing their ads to coincide with local paydays.

Begin to work today on mastering the three Rs. You may be amazed at the results you get when you get the right message to the right audience at the right time.

Chapter 2

Customer Service: How to Provide 24-Karat Care

Thousands of articles and hundreds of books have been written about customer service. However, the attention paid to winning and satisfying customers is more lip service than action. A friendly smile in every aisle, silky smooth voices on the telephone, and courteous employees are important, but you shouldn't confuse these bare-bones fundamentals with the real thing.

In this chapter you'll learn the difference between lip service and 24-karat customer care. I'll show you how to identify the five levels of customer service and move your company to the top. You'll read about two important customer service paradigms, afterservice and foreservice.

In addition, I've included tips on how to avoid losing customers and sales, and how to resolve complaints in five easy steps. You'll learn how to create a bionic workforce, and you'll learn to be wary of the polite customer.

With 24-karat care, you'll be set to take on any competitor and win. You will see customers in a new light—they will be as bright and exciting as a seam of gold illuminated by a miner's lamp.

More important, you'll know how to mine the gold by treating customers as if they were the only reason your business or job exists. Which, of course, is exactly what they are.

Improving Customer Care

Today, small businesses must stay completely focused on their customers if they are to survive. It takes superior customer service to hold market share and excellent service to gain on the pack. I'm not talking about lip service, but about real, honest-to-goodness customer care.

Based on conversations I've had with hundreds of business owners and customers around the country, I believe there are five levels of customer service. You may see your business as being at one of the levels we describe. If you're not where you would like to be, you may want to move your service quality up a notch.

Five Levels of Care

1. *No care.* The lowest level of customer service is no care. A 1994 study by Yankelovich Partners found that for many businesses, no care is the norm. Of the customers surveyed, 62 percent reported that they had walked out of a business because no one greeted them, waited on them, or offered to help. That's no care.

In the same survey, 60 percent of the respondents reported asking a question that the sales clerk couldn't answer. To make matters worse, most didn't offer to find out. That's no service.

2. *Barely care.* Barely care is the level at which many small businesses perform. They give barely any real customer service. They do almost nothing to set themselves apart from the megastores, which also provide barely care.

Businesses that give barely care greet their customers, offer assistance, and say thanks. Then they go on to the next sale. The previous customer is quickly forgotten as they repeat the process on the next one.

3. *Reactive care.* The business that gives reactive care provides barely care and then goes one step beyond. The additional step is to let the customer know someone is there to help if needed. The customer must take the initiative, but if the customer calls, he or she is assured of assistance.

Each of these steps is an improvement. Barely care is better than no care, and reactive care is better than barely care—barely.

4. *Proactive care.* Proactive care goes beyond reactive care. Businesses that give proactive care follow up with customers. They initiate calls to see how customers are doing.

Proactive care givers really are interested in ensuring that each customer's needs are being met. They want to serve the customer more effectively, because they know that the only way they can guarantee future business is to keep the customer satisfied.

Proactive care is a high level of customer service. However, if you're providing proactive care, you could still lose your customers to a competitor who goes all out to please them.

5. *Whatever-it-takes care.* Whatever-it-takes customer service includes the best of all other levels of service. In addition, it encompasses building a partnership with customers.

This level of service is not just based on giving great service to ensure the next sale, but also focuses on helping customers even if you don't make another sale. Your business becomes giving customers what they want and need.

Whatever-it-takes care will require a higher level of commitment and employee training than you've provided in the past. You'll have to stretch to build new relationships. You'll have to think like a partner with your customers. You'll have to know your customers' needs as well as you know your own.

The reward is customer loyalty. I know you've heard that customer loyalty doesn't exist anymore. For most businesses that is true. Most businesses don't offer whatever-it-takes care. No care equals no loyalty. Barely care, reactive care, and even proactive care offer little promise of "customers for life." Whatever-it-takes care will ensure satisfied customers who want to do business with you again and again.

Afterservice

We use the term *aftershocks* to describe tremors that occur after earthquakes. We say *afternoon* to define the hours following noon and preceding evening. We call the device that produces extra thrust in a jet engine an *afterburner*. From now on, we will use the term *afterservice* to describe service after the sale. Remember, you read it here first.

Afterservice is not a new concept. Several business articles have touched on the topic, and a few books on customer service offer a page or two on it in the back. Though it isn't a new concept, it isn't worn out from frequent use either. Like a well-maintained car, afterservice still has a lot of mileage left in it.

Business is changing rapidly in the 1990s. We are in an increasingly competitive environment. Competition comes from around the world, and catalog purveyors can capture your customers from across the country. Many companies are developing a stronger customer service focus. Afterservice may be one of the few ways left to distinguish your business from the rest of the pack.

Courting Customers

More years ago than I like to remember, I began dating my wife, Sue. We conducted the final year of our courtship long distance—I was working in Chicago, and Sue was completing college in Missouri.

Although I traveled the 453 miles to see her as often as I could, the time between our visits seemed unbearable. We shortened the days separating those visits with love-filled letters. Frequently, Sue would begin a letter within hours of our last embrace. She would be reaffirming her love for me while I made the seven-hour drive back to the city.

While our relationships with our customers are not usually as intense and emotional as our courtships, some parallels do exist. For example, acknowledgments of genuine appreciation and thanks after the sale are often as welcome as a loving note from a sweetheart.

Another similarity is found when customers are taken for granted. Customers who are not reminded of our appreciation are often vulnerable to the overtures of an aggressive competitor. In business, as in love, you may be the last to know.

There are three important aspects of afterservice: follow-up, follow-up, and follow-up. I'm a firm believer in the 80-20 rule. This rule states that 80 percent of your business comes from only 20 percent of your customers. If this rule applies to your firm, you might concentrate your initial follow-up on the top 20 percent of your accounts.

Afterservice Tips

The most important component in any afterservice program is keeping your promises. There is no better follow-up than doing exactly what you said you would do. We build and nurture all business relationships on trust. Keep your promises after the sale, and you'll keep the business.

Another afterservice tip is to make personal visits to see your best customers. You send a strong message when you make an in-person expression of your interest in, and appreciation for, your customers.

Phone follow-up is another accepted method. You don't need a crisis to call a customer. Sometimes a "thinking of you" phone call can lead to future business and improved customer relations.

Direct mail is another valid follow-up technique. Customers appreciate afterservice notes, letters, satisfaction surveys, and reply cards. Keep them brief and business-oriented. Thank-you cards are good as long as they don't get mushy. Many businesses use holiday cards, birthday cards, and special occasion cards effectively.

Why not give afterservice a try this afternoon? You may find that it kicks in your business's afterburner, and you may feel the aftershocks for months. Afterservice often leaves a pleasant aftertaste and afterimage afterward.

Foreservice

The ink was barely dry on the "afterservice" thought when the idea for this segment materialized. The topic came up in a casual conversation during a break in an "Up Against the Wal-Marts" workshop I was presenting.

Pat Reed planted the seed that sprouted into this idea. Reed is the director of operations for a buying group that provides services to retail appliance dealers in Missouri, Arkansas, Tennessee, and Mississippi. He and I were discussing the importance of providing service after the sale.

After agreeing there was a shortage of afterservice, Reed offered some additional insight. "Not only is there a limited supply of service after the sale, but there is also a shortage of service before the sale," he said. He added that smaller businesses can make up ground lost to the discounters and specialty chains by providing service before the sale. And that is how I got a brand new word for service before the sale: *foreservice.*

Afterservice and Foreservice

Most business owners recognize the importance of afterservice; however, what Reed was suggesting was that service before the sale was equally important, and also in short supply. I pondered that thought as I drove home from the workshop.

Here are some tips Reed and I came up with that may help you increase your customers' level of confidence and satisfaction before the sale. Use them to turn prospects into buyers, then use afterservice to keep those buyers satisfied.

Foreservice Tips

▪ *Get to know every customer.* Take time to learn your customers names and to find their interests. Customers like to do business with people they know—particularly the owner of the business. Ask questions to determine needs and qualify prospects. Don't underestimate the power of the personal touch.

- *Don't promise more than you can deliver.* You may make the sale this time, but you will probably lose the customer. The best approach is to underpromise and overdeliver. Remember, your reputation and integrity are on the line every time.

- *Be knowledgeable about your products and services.* You and every employee should gain product knowledge every day. One way to gain new customers is to "out-know" your competition. People are willing to pay more for knowledge and information. Many of the mass merchandisers and specialty chains are weak in this area. Take advantage of their weakness by making product knowledge your strength.

- *Stress the benefits of your products and services.* All customers want the following benefits: more time, more money, less aggravation, and enhanced feelings of self-worth. Clearly and concisely pointing out the advantages you offer is good foreservice.

- *Don't forget to be courteous.* Even if you can't fill every need, a friendly, courteous manner will bring the customers back again and again. Good foreservice includes a friendly greeting, a warm smile, and calling the customer by name, if you can.

- Foreservice also includes adjusting your store hours to suit your customers' preferences, creating cheerful and appealing displays of merchandise, and making it easy for customers' to contact you by providing twenty-four-hour hot lines or toll-free phone numbers.

Why not give foreservice a try today? I foresee that you will find yourself on the forefront of a business experience that will foreshadow greater sales ahead.

The Lost Sale

The mall was crowded, but the bookstore was almost empty. I was browsing through a stack of discounted books when a customer approached the nearby checkout counter.

After waiting a few moments, she interrupted the clerks, who were busily engaged in an animated, but private, conversation.

Finally, one of the clerks turned and offered to help. The customer asked if the store carried a particular book on a business topic. Without moving, the clerk said that she was sorry, but they didn't have that book in stock.

The clerk offered no additional assistance and returned to her interrupted conversation. The customer murmured her thanks and left the store with a disappointed look.

Ordinarily, I wouldn't have paid any attention to this none-of-my-business conversation. However, on this occasion, I had just examined a copy of the book in question—at least, I thought I had. My curiosity was aroused, and I returned to the business section. Four copies of the exact book the customer requested were on the shelf, available for sale.

The potential customer, however, was gone. The sale was lost. Everyone lost in this exchange. The customer's want was not satisfied. The owner's profits were not bolstered by the sale. Even the clerk lost. She lost an opportunity to serve a customer and a chance to increase her value as an employee. Finally, she allowed potential profit and additional job security to become a competitor's opportunity.

Preventing the Loss

In this case, the loss was preventable. The desired product was in the store, and the sale should have been made. This is not always true. However, even if the desired product is not in inventory, you may not lose the sale. There are ways to prevent losses.

First, everyone in the store should know the inventory. I know it is not humanly possible to memorize every one of the thousands of titles on a bookstore's shelves. However, in this case, a quick check on the store's computer would have shown that the book was in stock.

If there is no computer at your store, encourage your employees to get out from behind the counter during slow times and work the inventory. Straighten up shelves, move merchandise to new locations, or create new displays. The more everyone knows about the inventory, the more likely you are to make a sale.

Second, everyone should be trained regularly. Every employee who comes into contact with customers should understand the importance of taking care of those customers. Training will reinforce the concept that the customer is the only reason any business exists.

With proper training, each clerk in the bookstore would quickly turn to the computer to check on the desired book as a routine service to each customer. Also, a trip to the business section would have made the sale. If the product was not on the shelf, and not in the back room, a knowledgeable clerk might have offered to get the book via special order.

Third, an employee should suggest a suitable alternative for an out-of-stock product. In this case, the bookstore carried at least four or five other books on the same subject. The customer might have chosen one of them as a satisfactory substitute.

Finally, a trained clerk armed with inventory knowledge and a true desire to help the customer can suggest additional items to enhance the sale. Challenge your employees to look for additional items to suggest to each customer. McDonald's sells a lot of french fries and apple pies by offering or suggesting those items to its customers.

Turning a lost sale into a satisfied customer is a great business-building strategy. Grow your business by knowing your inventory, focusing on the customer, and using the power of suggestive selling.

Resolving Complaints

If you're in business, it's bound to happen to you—sooner or later, you will be accosted by an unhappy customer. The problem may be real or imagined. It may be of serious consequence or a simple misunderstanding. How you deal with angry and unhappy customers can put money in your pocket or send you to the poorhouse.

Research shows that each unhappy customer tells more than fifteen others about unsatisfactory service. Few small businesses can afford this type of negative publicity. Therefore, you must deal with problems quickly and sincerely.

Difficulties with customers often occur when the customers feel cheated or believe that you didn't live up to your end of the bargain. Because of previous bad experiences, they may feel that you won't care about their problems.

Often, these customers are angry and ready to unload on you or your company. They may think you won't listen unless they show you how upset they are.

Angry customers require careful handling. However, there are no better customers than the ones whose problems you resolve. They become a steady, reliable source of income for your business. These customers know you will take good care of them if a problem arises.

We Have a Problem

The first step toward solving any problem is acknowledging its existence. Don't try to deny that the situation exists. If your customer believes there is a problem, there is a problem. It may not be your fault, but you must still find a solution. When you acknowledge the difficult situation, you begin to drain off steam, which may keep the customer from exploding. You can help by staying calm yourself.

The second step is to listen patiently to the customer. An angry customer needs to vent some frustration. By being a patient listener, you accomplish two things: You allow the customer to work off some anger, and you begin gathering facts and details about what went wrong.

After the customer has lowered his or her adrenaline level, try to find the real cause of dissatisfaction. This may take some probing. Once you find the source of unhappiness, you're a step closer to finding a solution.

Find the Facts

Engage in a fact-finding dialogue. Ask relevant questions. Make certain you know what happened and when. It doesn't hurt to make some notes at this point. When customers see you writing down their comments, they may stick a little more closely to the facts. Your notes also serve as a record in case you cannot resolve the problem right away.

Once you have all the information, move quickly to resolve the complaint. Ask the customer to propose a solution. If the desired action is realistic, do it. Replace the item, refund the money, or fix the product.

Nordstrom stores are known around the world for their outstanding customer service. All store employees receive training in resolving complaints. It is no accident that Nordstrom has ranked number one in customer service for years.

If you cannot solve the problem immediately, let the customer know what you are going to do. You must communicate any progress to the customer. Postponing the problem is not a solution. Remember, the goal of resolving complaints is to create a satisfied customer.

The Bionic Workforce

It is not a new idea. It is not new technology. In fact, bionic workforces have been around for centuries. The evidence for this is the many high-quality products whose bionic craftsmanship has lasted for hundreds of years.

I realize I may have confused some of you who were big fans of the *Six Million Dollar Man* television series. You are thinking of bionics in terms of electromechanically enhanced body parts. However, the bionic workforces I'm talking about existed long before electricity and medical science got together.

I first learned about the true meaning of *bionic* a few weeks ago from Don and Glenda Carper, the co-owners of Doodles Hamburgers Inc. Glenda was preparing a workforce training program for employees and was kind enough to share her thoughts with me. As soon as I heard her discuss the subject, I knew I should pass her ideas along to you.

The Meaning of Bionic

Glenda's training program uses an acronym built from the word *bionic*. The letters introduce the phrase "Believe It Or Not, I Care." Bionic service is pretty rare these days. In fact, when you run across a company or an employee who really cares, it stands out because it is so unusual.

It is a shame that caring companies and employees are scarce, but it is true. Every business owner has glorious opportunities to grow his or her business by providing caring service. People love to go where they are treated well.

My family and I often travel together on business trips. We see many examples of employees who have forgotten their bionic training or were never taught to care in the first place.

A memorable example of poor service and lack of a bionic attitude occurred a few months ago at a fast-food restaurant. We arrived at 10:05 A.M. with the intention of ordering a quick breakfast. At 10:25 A.M., when we were still standing in a slow-moving line, an employee announced that the restaurant was no longer serving breakfast.

Although the store was busy, the employees were standing around waiting for someone else to do something. The place was not nearly as clean as other stores in the chain, and there was a lot more conversation than activity. This crew needed a bionic attitude.

Low-Level Service

A second memorable example of the need for bionic training happened on the same trip as we flew home. We boarded the plane, and it was obvious to me that the plane would not be full. Since the airline assigns seats on its airplanes, I asked the flight attendant for permission to take one of the empty seats. She replied, "Sir, the plane will be full; you will have to sit in your assigned seat." She said it firmly, and without a smile.

As we settled snugly together in our seats, I offered to bet my family that the plane wouldn't be full. The flight attendant must have been standing right behind me because she stepped up and repeated curtly that the plane would be full.

A few minutes later, as we backed from the gate, I counted eleven empty seats in the three rows directly in front of me. Later in the flight, the attendant told me it was all right to move to an empty row if I wanted. I told her my present seat was fine. What I didn't tell her was that the seat was OK, but I would choose a different airline for my next flight. The airline's slogan, "We love to fly and it shows," must not be based on bionic service.

Caring workforces can make a difference. Try developing a "Believe It Or Not, I Care" attitude and watch your business or career grow.

No Service, No Sale

We've all seen the signs near the entries of business establishments that say, NO SHIRT, NO SHOES, NO SERVICE. Based on some of the stories I've heard, I believe it is time for a new sign. When we enter a store as a customer, we should wear a large sign around our necks that says NO SERVICE, NO SALE.

The intent of this sign is to remind business owners that if we don't receive good service, we'll take our business elsewhere. Of course, that is exactly what we do anyway. The sign might help those who want our business remember what happens when customers don't receive good service.

Over the years, hundreds of books have been written on the subject of customer service. Thousands of articles have been published, and I have even written a few *Minding Your Own Business* newspaper columns on the topic. Yet, it is still one of the most neglected areas of small-business management.

The following true experiences were all related to me by disappointed customers. They are good examples of no service, no sale.

Taken to the Cleaners

A dry-cleaning establishment in an area convenient to Larry's daily travels reopened under new management. The manager was enthusiastic and invited Larry to give the store a try.

Since the store was nearby, Larry dropped off two suits for dry cleaning and some shirts for laundering. A few days later, he picked up the items on his way to the airport. He was flying to a nearby state to give an important presentation.

When Larry began to dress for his presentation the following day, he found that the suit he planned to wear was not clean. The other suit was clean, but not pressed. Obviously, he was not a happy camper.

When Larry returned home, he explained the problem to the manager. The manager took his phone number and promised to have the owner call. "There was never an apology or an offer to do the job right," Larry said. "I wasn't asked to bring the clothes in again, nor was I offered a refund. Two weeks have passed, and I've had no telephone call." Larry has found a new cleaner. No service, no sale.

More Nonservice

Sue picked out an expensive bridal gift from the bridal registry of a national department store. The store is upscale and pricey. She expected good service there.

Later, when she received no thank-you note from the bride, Sue inquired of the bride's family, who told her that the gift was never delivered. When Sue returned to the store, a clerk informed her flatly and rudely that the computer said that the bride had received the gift and computers do not lie. Sue hasn't darkened their door since. No service, no sale.

Sandra wanted some remodeling done in her home. She called a contractor friend, who promised to come out and look at the job "within the next two weeks." After three weeks passed, Sandra called again. "Within the week," the contractor promised.

Two more weeks passed, and Sandra phoned again. Her friend made several excuses and again promised to come look at the job "in the next couple of weeks." Finally, Sandra saw another contractor's ad in her newspaper and called. This contractor came out the next evening and took detailed notes on the work Sandra wanted done. He returned the following day with a detailed written bid and references. Sandra checked the references, then authorized the work.

"My new room is beautiful," she said. "However, I don't really know what to tell my contractor friend when he calls." I guess Sandra could say, "No service, no sale."

Missed Opportunities

The clerk didn't look up as I entered the motel lobby. I approached the counter, and without making eye contact the clerk said, "Yes?"

"I'm Don Taylor, and I hope you have a room reserved for me," I replied. The clerk frowned and marked his place carefully in the stack of papers he was working on. He checked the records and slapped a registration form on the counter. "Fill out the top part," the clerk ordered. There was no please, no greeting, no smile, no eye contact, just the order to fill out the form.

I filled out the card and asked politely, "That is a non-smoking room, isn't it?"

"Yes," was the short reply.

"If you have something on the ground floor I'd appreciate it," I suggested hopefully. I'd just driven 350 miles after a full day at the office, and the thought of making several trips upstairs was not appealing.

"No," he replied. "Your room is on the second floor."

I sighed and reminded myself that it was late and the motel was probably full, and I should be grateful just to have a room. I accepted the key and followed the perfunctory instructions for finding my room.

As I parked, I noticed that several ground-floor non-smoking rooms were empty. That was when I realized that I was more of an interruption to the motel clerk's work than a customer to be pleased. Changing my room from the second floor to the first would have required a computer entry and would have added to his end-of-shift paperwork.

The following morning I was greeted by a somewhat more friendly clerk. As I checked out, she pushed a brochure into my hand. "This is your 'Return Club' membership," she said. "It's good for a free night's stay." I took the brochure, said thank you to the clerk, and thought to myself, "It would have to be free if I stay here again."

Later I looked at the brochure. If I gave the motel chain more than seventy pieces of personal data, including salary and credit information, and stayed eleven nights, I could earn a free room. " 'Earn' is the right word," I thought as I threw away the brochure.

Giving Business Away

Later that day, I shared this experience with seventy-five business owners and managers. I was conducting a business development workshop, and this missed opportunity was a perfect illustration of how poor customer service drives away future business.

The night clerk didn't really care about my business. I was an interruption. It didn't matter if I got what I wanted, as long as I didn't cause him any extra work. Getting his paperwork done was more important than satisfying my needs.

The sad part of this story is that it's repeated thousands of times each day. Millions of future sales are lost by businesses everywhere because employees have "I don't care" attitudes.

I'm certain that many people were involved in putting together this national motel chain's frequent-customer promotion. I'm sure hundreds of thousands of dollars were spent on brochures and advertising. It's a shame to see a portion of that effort wasted because of one clerk's attitude. It was a missed opportunity.

Business is a series of ongoing opportunities: chances to serve customers, deliver quality products or services, and exceed customers' expectations. Every day we're blessed with hundreds of such opportunities.

We may miss some of these opportunities because of aggressive competitors. We may miss others because of price or cost factors that are beyond our control. However, the missed opportunities that wreck our business are those we have control over—those caused by factors like customer service. When you drive business away, the result is truly missed opportunities.

The Polite Customer

I usually don't write when I'm irritated. However, I'll make an exception this time. It is 6:37 A.M., and I'm an unhappy customer.

I'm sitting in my car waiting for the fast-food restaurant's drive-through window to open so that I can order a quick breakfast. The sign promised that the restaurant would start serving at 6:30 A.M.

Because I'm a polite customer, I've waited seven minutes without honking. I'll just sit here until the restaurant gets around to opening.

Usually I'm not easily irritated. However, as I pulled in this morning, I did notice the employees standing around talking. They are not concerned that I'm waiting outside. I get breakfast here nearly every morning, and they know that I'll wait patiently until they turn on the lights. Then I'll order politely, as usual.

Not a Complainer

I have never complained. I didn't even complain last week when they put the wrong breakfast biscuit in my bag. It wasn't what I ordered, but I didn't discover the mistake until I was miles up the road. I didn't go back and raise Cain. I wasn't raised that way. My mother taught me to eat what was served and not to cause a big scene. I really am a polite customer.

I don't fuss when I have to ask twice for strawberry jelly. I always say thanks when I finally do get what I order. I don't even mind too much when they forget my straw or the napkins. I just drink out of the cup and use one of the spare napkins I keep in the glove box.

I don't complain when they partially fill my cup with Dr Pepper before remembering that I ordered Diet Coke. I just drink the mixture although I have never cared for the taste of Dr Pepper. Life is too short to quibble over a little thing like that.

Last week, when the sleepy drive-through person handed out a cup dripping excess cola down the side, I took it graciously. I wiped it off in the car and hoped it hadn't dripped all over my suit, shirt, and upholstery. I may have frowned when this happened, but I didn't complain. I really am a polite customer.

Equal Rights

Of course, business owners have the right to open whenever they please. They have a right to open late, fill orders incorrectly, and give mediocre service.

However, the advantage of living in America is that customers have rights, too. I have a right to spend my money at the business of my choice. I have a right to expect a business to keep its promises. Therefore, I expect this restaurant to open promptly at 6:30 A.M. That is what the sign promises. I also expect to get exactly what I ordered, and fast, friendly service. That is implied.

I may be a polite customer now, but I can become something else. I can become an ex-customer. I may quietly drive away and never come in again.

I may have to go out of my way, but I'll find a place that really cares about my business. A place where the employees strive to get the order right every time. Yesterday I noticed a restaurant that's open twenty-four hours every day. I wouldn't have to wait for it to open. I wonder what its breakfast biscuits taste like.

There are millions of nice, polite customers just like me. With our dollars, we will vote some businesses out of business this year. Maybe we're not so polite after all.

It is ironic when you think about it. Businesses will spend thousands of dollars in advertising this year just to replace customers who finally got fed up. This is money that could have been saved by giving timely, accurate, friendly service.

Chapter 3

Financial Management: Turning Gold Into Dollars and Dollars Into Sense

If you understand how our basic economic system works, you can increase your income, raise your standard of living, and enjoy greater job stability. The keys to making sense of dollars are simple: You must learn about financial management, then fully understand our free-enterprise economy, and, finally, know how to track and analyze relevant financial information.

In this chapter, I will introduce you to simple, easy-to-use ways to increase income, understand the difference between profit and cash flow, find where cash can hide in a business, and avoid credit problems. You'll get a dose of "dog-and-flea economics," and learn how to collect your accounts receivable like a pro.

I'll show you the difference between symptoms and real problems. You'll learn how to keep more of the money you earn, and how to earn more with what you keep. I'll prove that by paying yourself first, you can secure your financial future.

The only good way to make money that I know of is to work for it. The only good way to attain wealth that I know first to make your money work for you. Ben Franklin was right: A penny saved really is a penny earned.

Perking Up Profits

Clem and Elmer were chewing and chatting on the front porch of the little country store. "Watermelons," said Elmer. "That's where the money is—big, juicy, Black Diamond watermelons."

"How's that?" asked Clem.

"Well," Elmer said, "we can go down south and buy a pickup load and bring 'em back up here to sell!"

"I've got a pickup and $40," said Clem, with excitement rising in his voice. "Let's do it."

And so the partnership began. An idea, combined with capital and labor, was brought to fruition by the desire for profit.

Clem gassed up the pickup, and they headed down south to buy a load of watermelons. They wangled a deal with a farmer to purchase the melons at ten for a dollar.

They drove back home and found a busy corner under a big shade tree. They put up a large sign that read FRESH WATERMELONS—10 CENTS.

In no time at all the melons sold out. Clem and Elmer grinned as they counted their money. However, the grins faded when they realized that after taking out their lunch expenses and gas for the pickup, they had a little less than when they started.

These two old country boys were nobody's fools. They figured, talked, and studied the situation. Finally, they reached a decision. The solution was a bigger truck.

Deadly Error

Clem and Elmer aren't the only ones to experience the "bigger truck" syndrome. It frequently happens when business owners focus on increasing sales instead of examining all aspects of the business for profitability.

This can be a deadly error. Unless there are adequate margins to support the growth, increasing sales may only make the potential loss greater.

Having accurate, frequent financial statements is a prerequisite for managing for profit. There are five key pieces of information to know:

1. Sales or revenues
2. Cost of goods sold
3. Gross profit
4. Operating or fixed expenses
5. Net income

Gross profit is determined by subtracting the cost of goods sold from sales. Net income is calculated by subtracting the operating expenses from the gross profit.

Increasing Profits

There are three basic ways of increasing profits:

1. Eliminate costs
2. Increase margins
3. Increase sales—if there is an adequate margin

The best way to improve profitability is to eliminate unnecessary costs. You can trim the cost of goods sold by finding less expensive raw materials, parts, and inventory. Buying groups and cooperatives may help in this area. You can also negotiate quantity discounts, payment terms, and free delivery from your current suppliers.

You can often reduce costs in fixed or operating expenses, as well. Trim insurance premiums by raising the deductible portion or eliminating unnecessary coverage. Renegotiate your lease. Hire quality employees—they always cost less in the long run. Shop around for every major purchase, and don't take any cost for granted.

The saying, "Use it up, wear it out, make do, or do without," is a good cost-elimination strategy. If something isn't essential, don't spend your profits on it.

The second method of increasing profits is to improve the gross profit margin. You can widen margins by increasing prices or reducing the cost of goods sold. Once you have trimmed costs, take a good look at your pricing structure. The right price is the highest price that competition and your customers will allow. Of course, the most important considerations are that your price must cover all costs and provide value for your customer.

The third method of increasing profits is to generate more sales. This works only when there is gross profit. Clem and Elmer's problem was that they were selling melons with no margin to cover their operating expenses. They might have produced a significant net income by pricing their melons at 15 to 20 cents each.

Focus some of your attention on sales numbers, but also watch costs and margins. Sales get you into business, but profits keep you there.

Cashing In

Running a small business is a lot like playing the casinos in Las Vegas. It is a gamble. As in Las Vegas, there are many losers. There is also the opportunity for gain, and some business players even hit it big.

There is another similarity: When you're out of cash, you're out of the game. Keeping a close eye on your cash flow can stretch your playing time. It can also ensure long-term success.

Cash flow is an often-misunderstood business management topic. Many owners and managers have difficulty distinguishing between cash flow and profitability. Many small companies are caught in the trap of being profitable, but out of cash.

Cash flow is defined as the actual movement of funds into and out of the business during any given period. Money comes into the business when cash sales are made, accounts receivable are collected, loans are acquired, or additional investment is added. Money flows out as bills are paid, owner's wages are drawn, taxes are deposited, loans are repaid, and so on.

Profit or net income is the portion left after all expenses are subtracted from revenues. Some of the confusion between profit and cash flow is the difference between expenses allowed by the IRS and items for which checks have to be written.

Depreciation is a good example. The IRS allows businesses to deduct depreciation of assets owned by the business as an expense. This lowers the amount of taxable income, but does not affect the cash flow of the business. No cash is actually paid out.

Loan principal repaid is another example of a difference between profit and cash flow. The interest portion of loan payments is allowed as a deduction by the IRS. The principal is not an expense and is not deductible. However, since a check is written for the full payment, the entire amount flows out of the business. Therefore, both principal and interest should be shown on the cash-flow statement.

Begin With the Basics

The first step in understanding cash-flow management is to understand the three basic financial statements. The balance sheet, the profit and loss statement, and the cash-flow statement each represent a different view of your business. By looking at all three dimensions, you can see what is happening in the business.

The balance sheet lists what the company owns (assets) and what the value of those assets comes from (owner's investment, loans, and retained earnings). The balance sheet derives its name from the accounting equation: Assets = liabilities + owner's equity. The assets owned must balance the amount owed by the company (debt) when added to the entrepreneur's ownership (equity).

The profit and loss statement includes noncash items, such as depreciation. It measures the total amount of income, minus expenses, over the accounting period. Usually, profit and loss statements are prepared on a monthly, quarterly, or annual basis.

The third financial statement that every company should have is the cash-flow statement. The cash-flow statement adds the perspective of cash inflows and outflows. It may be the most valuable statement in giving a total picture of the company's finances.

For example, a retail gift shop may have nearly one-half of its annual sales volume in the final quarter. A lawn and garden center will generate the bulk of its sales in the spring. Both may show profits, but the negative cash flow they experience during certain seasons can cause problems if planning doesn't take into account the actual flow of cash in and out of the business.

Entrepreneurs are human in their habit of "spending what you have." By analyzing all three financial statements, you can understand what is really happening inside your business. You will also be able to anticipate any cash-flow problems and make necessary adjustments.

Cash gives you more flexibility in playing the game. Above all, it keeps you *in* the game.

Don't Get Left Holding the Bag

Kevin and Marci's business was doing well. Sales in their appliance and electronics store were up nearly 15 percent over last year. They were justifiably proud of that increase because the economy in their community was very slow.

Kevin was especially pleased with the new line of business he had generated. Though it had taken months of work, he had convinced several local home builders to install his premium appliance brands.

One large contractor had been tough to sell. Finally, he had agreed to place his business with Kevin and Marci in return for extended credit terms. Marci was concerned because the terms more than doubled their average accounts receivable.

Kevin didn't allow Marci's fears to dampen his spirits. Although a few months earlier the local rumor mill had suggested that this builder had financial troubles, Kevin thought the potential sales justified the risk. After all, he pointed out to Marci, they were getting nearly the full markup on sales to this account.

For several months events proceeded smoothly. The contractor placed large orders, and though his was a slow-paying account, his checks were always good. Kevin didn't think too much about the sudden resignation of the builder's comptroller.

Less than a week later, a tearful Marci ran into the store waving the local newspaper. "I knew it was too good to be true," she cried, pointing at the day's top story. The headline read, "Local Contractor Files for Bankruptcy." Kevin's heart sank as they checked their books. The contractor's account contained nearly $40,000 in unpaid receivables.

Warning Signals

Take a good look at all of your open-account customers. If any of them filed for bankruptcy protection, would it place your business in jeopardy? Has competition or your desire for sales pushed you into a position of extending more credit than you would like?

If you answered yes to either of the above questions, take heed. If you are going to assume the role of banker for any of your customers, you need to be aware of the pitfalls. Unexpected bankruptcies really do happen.

You can lower your risk by establishing tough credit policies and watching for financial warning signals. Here are six danger signs:

1. *Negative gossip in the local rumor mill.* While you shouldn't believe everything you hear, persistent rumblings about one of your open, unsecured accounts should get your attention. Pull a current credit report, request up-to-date financial statements, and watch closely for any changes.
2. *Key personnel turnover.* Kevin should have been concerned by the abrupt resignation of the builder's comptroller. To use an old-time analogy, rats often jump off a sinking ship.
3. *IRS problems, tax and mechanics liens, and legal actions.* These often signal that a customer is in trouble. Check with the courthouse or the recorder of deeds for such filings. Some problems may not show up on a credit report.
4. *Slower-than-usual, partial, or sporadic payments.* This may be an early tipoff of cash-flow problems. Monitor all of your open accounts. An aging of receivables report can help you spot changes in payment patterns.
5. *Lack of communication.* This is a danger signal. You should be concerned about phone calls that are never returned, letters that go unanswered, and key personnel who dodge any attempt to be contacted. False information should also cause alarm. The check shouldn't be in the mail for too long.
6. *An increasing volume of business.* This may be good news or bad news. Sometimes when a business that is a poor credit risk is cut off by some of its suppliers, it will be forced to place business wherever it can. Watch out for large orders and unexplained increases.

As with many other problems, early recognition may prevent loss. Look for warning signals, and don't get stuck holding the bag.

Dog-and-Flea Economics

The best thing about having a post office box is the pleasant surprises you find in it. I had one of these some time ago when I found a letter from Phil Schlarb, an old friend who lives near Trenton, Missouri.

Schlarb is a professor and part-time dean at North Central Missouri College. He is also a successful entrepreneur. His approach to teaching business and economics courses is an appropriate and interesting blend of common sense and classic business theory. Schlarb exposes students to a hearty dose of the way the world really works.

Therefore, it was with great interest that I read the five-page essay he included with his letter. Schlarb wrote the piece, titled "Dog-and-Flea Economics," to show students the importance of studying economics.

Schlarb contends in his essay that those who learn how our economic system works can raise their standard of living, increase their income, and enjoy greater job stability. I agree, and I felt that many of you would enjoy his creative way of looking at economics.

Of Dogs and Fleas

Schlarb compares our economy to the relationship of a dog and its fleas. We are all economic fleas, he contends, and we share our dog's fortune. The good news is that you get to pick your own dog. The bad news is that you have little or no control over your dog.

Economic dogs include your profession, your education, your employer, and the world economy. You may have to change dogs from time to time to maintain your economic prosperity.

Schlarb points to several cases from our nation's history in which economic change made some of us find a new dog. For example, the development of double-knit fabric resulted in the closing of 50 percent of our nation's dry cleaners. The employees—economic fleas—didn't do anything wrong, but they were still in trouble when their dog died.

Refrigeration killed the icebox and block ice industries, but generated great employment in manufacturing and servicing refrigerators and freezers. The electronic calculator retired the slide rule, but increased the number of people working in the electronics industry. The point: Old dogs die and new ones are born. It is as natural in economics as it is in dogdom.

Schlarb ends his essay with some thought-provoking concepts:

Points to Ponder

- *Only people have expenses.* Neither businesses nor governments have expenses. These institutions simply pass costs on to the consumer or taxpayer.

- *Only people create opportunities for businesses.* Schlarb points to the vacant buildings in many rural towns with declining populations as an example. The businesses previously housed in those now-empty buildings are dead because when people move away, they take their dollars with them.

- *Risk and profit travel together.* The willingness to accept risk separates the entrepreneur from the spectators. Many people have good ideas, but few are willing to risk time, money, and their reputation. Respect those who accept risk, because without them there would be little progress.

- *What's good for one may be bad for others.* A snowstorm may slow traffic for many retailers, but it will spur sales of tire chains, snow blowers, and insulated boots. Consumers will welcome a new Wal-Mart store, but other business owners may greet it with fear and hate.

- *There ain't no free lunch.* Everything costs something, and there are both direct costs and opportunity costs. Economics is basically a study of how people, companies, and countries decide to spend their money and time.

Collecting

Larry is a successful small-business owner whose sales are increasing steadily. In May, he achieved his third record month in a row. Business is booming, but Larry's bank account is empty. Selling is becoming easier, but Larry is slow in collecting the money his credit customers owe him.

Like Larry, many businesses are selling on credit. We're not talking about credit card sales; rather, we mean open-account, unsecured credit. When you sell on credit, you are not only in the selling business, but also in the collection business. This is an area of business that many entrepreneurs struggle with.

Laura is a perfect illustration of this point. Laura runs a very successful service business. She is bright, talented, and pleasant. Her work is excellent, and her prices are reasonable.

Laura came to us for help because she was out of cash. Sales were strong and she had more work than she could do, but she had no cash and couldn't pay some of her suppliers.

The first thing we did was analyze Laura's financial records to see if she had a profitability problem or a cash-flow problem. Upon examining Laura's business records, we found that she was generating profit, but she wasn't collecting cash from her customers quickly enough. The result was that Laura was using her available cash to pay the higher variable expenses that come with increased sales. It was a classic cash-flow problem.

In Laura's case, we made several recommendations for improving collection and cash flow. Here are several tips that you can use, too:

Improving Collection

• *Send out your bills quickly.* When Laura landed new clients and got very busy, her billing regularity slipped. Sometimes accounts went for as long as forty-five days without receiving a bill.

Our experience has been that even your best-paying accounts won't pay until they receive a bill. If you're experiencing cash-flow problems, we recommend that you send out bills as soon as you complete the work.

▪ *Bill frequently.* On jobs where you don't complete the work quickly, make partial billings. Bill on the fifteenth and the thirtieth of each month. Billing quickly and more frequently will improve cash flow.

▪ *Bill clearly and accurately.* Inaccurate or unclear invoices will always delay your collection process. To ensure clarity, keep bills simple and uncomplicated. Describe each billing item separately.

Check your math. Double-check all figures and calculations. Make certain that all bills are based on accurate charges. You may wish to provide documentation of delivery or services rendered.

▪ *Bill conveniently.* Enclose a self-addressed envelope. Make it easy for the person you've billed to pay your bill. Although simple, this technique may move your invoice to the top of the "to be paid" pile.

▪ *Expect prompt payment.* Once you've sent an accurate bill, you have a right to expect prompt, timely payment. If you don't receive that payment within a reasonable period, communicate your expectation clearly. Don't delay. Get on the phone and let your customer know that you expect payment.

If you're not going to get paid, it is better to know now. You may want to take quick action, such as canceling further work orders or shipments.

▪ *Follow up.* No one likes to make collection calls. It is stressful. It is not fun. However, it's no fun not being able to pay your bills either.

When you must make collection calls, get right to the point. Don't beat around the bush and don't apologize for calling. You shouldn't be on the defensive. You have a right to be paid and you need to express it. Follow your call with a short letter confirming your conversation. You'll be pleased with the results.

What's the Problem?

"What's the problem?" my doctor asked. So I described my aches and pains. "What's the problem?" my mechanic asked. I told him how my car was clicking and grinding. "What's the problem?" I asked a recent small-business client. "I don't have any money, and it's really a problem!" the client replied.

What do these three scenarios have in common? In all three cases the question "What's the problem?" was answered with a description of symptoms.

Symptoms are visible or discernible indications of problems. They are observable signs, conditions, or events. Symptoms can be irritating, painful, or confusing. However, they are not in and of themselves the real problem.

You may have chronic shoulder pain because you've torn a muscle, you've dislocated the joint, or you have arthritis. The pain is the symptom; the cause of the pain is the problem. Likewise, the grinding noise in my car is not the problem, but rather the result of an impending mechanical failure.

However, when it comes to business, we often see not having any money as the problem. When we're broke or experiencing severe cash-flow problems, we usually seek to borrow money to solve the problem. This is a little like treating a brain tumor with megadoses of aspirin. The symptom of pain may disappear briefly, but the problem still exists.

Looking for the Source

The key to finding the real problem is to begin looking for the cause or source of your difficulty. In business, there are two main reasons for being cash deficient: not being profitable and having cash tied up in inappropriate places.

Let's look at the profitability problem first. The selling price of your product or service must cover all your costs. This includes the variable costs (the cost of goods or services sold) and the fixed costs (the operating expenses that are not directly related to your sales). If your costs are greater than your sales, you will sell yourself out of cash very quickly. Your options are to increase your selling price, thereby creating more margin, or cut costs, which will leave more dollars for the bottom line.

The second problem is one of insufficient or diverted cash flow. Examine your revenues and costs. If you determine that you have profit, but you're out of cash, then you may have an actual cash-flow deficit.

Remember, when you're short of cash, the shortage is the result of other actions, conditions, or events. It is the symptom, not the actual problem. The key is to know where cash can hide in your business.

There are three places in a business where cash can be. It can hide in inventory. It can sneak into accounts receivable. It can also disguise itself as fixed assets, such as new vehicles, equipment, furniture, and fixtures.

None of these conditions is bad in and of itself. Growing your inventory may help you increase sales and improve profits. Increasing accounts receivable levels will logically follow improving sales. New equipment may make your operation more efficient and productive, leading to even greater profit.

However, excessive use of cash in these areas can bring about cash shortages. Therefore, track your inventory closely, watch your receivables, and consider long-term financing for capital equipment or vehicle purchases in order to keep your cash flow in hand.

If you don't discover the root problem by examining profitability, checking inventory and receivable levels, and monitoring capital expenditures, there are two other causes for cash shortages. The first is excessive drawing (salary) by the owner or owners, the second is shrinkage or theft. Remember to look for the cause so that you can correct the problem, not just temporarily relieve the symptom.

Keeping Your Dollars

There was a time when I preferred playing softball to eating. For several years, I led our fast-pitch team in batting average and RBIs. One of the first lessons I learned as a hitter was to keep my eye on the ball. In the world of fast-pitch softball, if you look away or even blink after the pitcher has started the windup, you're an easy out.

In the world of small business, the same principle applies. You must stay alert so that you can take your best swing in any situation.

This is especially true in the area of keeping and managing the dollars you've earned. We frequently counsel business owners and managers whose businesses are profitable. However, they often complain that there is never enough cash. The money came in during the month, but now it's gone.

The first step in getting a handle on where the money goes is to examine your expenses. Cost control keeps your dollars working for you, but it is only one part of a good financial management policy.

Financial management is a process that uses the numbers generated by a business for making business decisions. The numbers come from accounting records and financial statements. Good record keeping is a prerequisite to good financial management.

Keep Your Eye on the Ball

Even if you have good records and financial statements, it is hard to stay alert. Cost control is an especially difficult area for small businesses.

The most common reason why costs rise is that we relax and look away. We let up in financial management to pay some attention to our marketing program. We take our eye off the cost ball—strike one.

Costs have a way of growing unnoticed. Several years ago, I worked as an independent consultant for a small business. The owner was concerned because the supply of money was short. The company was growing, but there was very little available cash after the monthly bills were paid.

A close examination of the records showed that several costs had risen for no apparent reason. Janitorial expenses had doubled, the cost of supplies had nearly tripled, and the telephone bills were out of sight. Within a week, the owner and I chopped nearly $3,000 from the monthly operating budget.

Pay What You Owe

Another area with which small businesses struggle is the payment of taxes. My philosophy here is to pay what you owe, but not a penny more. Many business owners are guilty of letting deductions and write-offs slip through their fingers. If you take your eye off the tax ball, it's a sure strike two.

Unless you are a certified public accountant or a tax specialist, you need to involve a professional in this area. Don't mess with the Internal Revenue Service. Have someone who is a business tax specialist do your returns.

Get advice early. You cannot always accomplish tax reduction at the end of the year. Careful consideration of purchases, leases, and expenditures at the beginning of the year can result in considerable tax savings. Don't strike out because you took your eye off the financial ball.

It's Your Money

You've always worked hard for your money. You have never lived extravagantly, but there never seems to be enough cash to make ends meet. You're still years away from retirement, but you haven't even thought of starting a serious savings program yet.

If you find saving money a tough job, you're in good company. Most Americans rank saving money at the top of

their "need to do" list. However, in reality, it scores near the
bottom of the "are doing" list. The New York Institute of
Finance reports that only 3 percent of the people who reach
retirement age are financially secure.

This year, why not make a commitment to begin your
journey to personal financial success and security? There is no
easy way, no thirty-day quick fix, and no miracle formula.
However, there are some time-proven principles that have
been used with success for hundreds of years. They can work
for you today.

Stay With a Plan

Most experts recommend beginning with a financial
plan. Start with a list of items worth saving for. You should
include short-, intermediate-, and long-term goals. For example, saving $2,000 for a summer vacation is a short-term goal.
Money for a preteen's college is an intermediate-term need,
and retirement funds would be long-term.

By establishing financial goals, you give yourself a target
to aim for. Now you can begin to direct your money toward
your goals.

At the top of every financial plan should be paying off all
debt. Thomas Fuller said, "Debt is the worst poverty." Publil-
ius Syrus said, "Debt is the slavery of the free." Thomas Jefferson said, "Never spend your money before you have it."

One of the most common and most debilitating forms of
debt is the infamous credit card. The interest rates can soar to
more than 20 percent per year. You can't afford to pay 20 percent interest. Pay off your charge cards. Don't charge more on
them. Reduce the number you hold and thereby the tempta-
tion to use them.

Pay Yourself First

You can save only if you put money into savings first. You
usually spend what you have left after paying the bills. To get

your savings started, take money out of your paycheck first. The amount is not really as important as establishing the habit.

You may set a goal of saving $200,000 over the next thirty years. A monthly deposit of $142, earning 8 percent interest, would accomplish that goal.

Another good way to save is to shorten the length of repayment terms. For example, a thirty-year, $50,000, 8 percent home mortgage has a monthly payment of $366.89. If you shorten the term of repayment to fifteen years, the payment grows to $477.83 per month, an increase of only $111. However, you save a whopping $46,071 in interest costs by shortening the term of the loan.

Now carry this little exercise a step further. Let's assume you pay off the mortgage in fifteen years and continue to deposit $477.83 into savings for another fifteen years. Earning 6 percent, your savings account would grow to more than $136,000.

In both cases you own your home free and clear. The extra $111 per month advanced your long-term savings by more than $136,000. So shorten the term and continue the payments.

The same principle will work for cars. Drive your paid-for car for three more years and make a $300 monthly deposit to savings. At the end of three years you'll have accumulated $11,700 to put down on your next car.

In summary: Plan, get out of debt, pay your savings first, and shorten repayment terms. It's your money, why not keep more of it?

Chapter 4

Starting Your Business: Prospecting for Gold

More than 80 percent of the people who start a business fail before the business reaches five years of age. Like prospectors lost in the desert, they wander aimlessly, looking for signs of wealth. Often a single turn takes them off the path that leads to the potential mother lode.

If you are in business now, have failed in business already, or are one of the more than 70 million Americans who wants to own your own business, I wrote this chapter for you. I'll disclose my secret source for business start-up information and show you where to dig for start-up gold.

You'll be granted a license to steal, and I'll show you how to use it legally and ethically. You'll learn a new bedtime story, "Goldilocks and the Three Barriers," and I'll help you answer the often-asked question, "Do I really have what it takes to start my own business?"

I'll discuss buying an existing business and help you determine a fair value. You'll learn how to pick a name that will help you grow your business, and how to be home-based and happy if that is your desire. So, grab your pick and shovel and let's get started.

My Secret Source

Nearly every working day, a client asks me a question I cannot answer. That can be a challenge when you are paid to answer questions and solve business problems. I have a secret source for the information I need, and I'm going to share it with you who purchased this book. The best place I know to get answers and information is at your local library.

General Information

Start at the reference desk. Your reference librarian will help you locate company information, demographics, and vital statistics. For example, if you are looking for information on national companies, several directories and resource books are available. Some of the publications that will be very beneficial in your search include *Standard & Poor's Register of Corporations, Dun & Bradstreet's Million Dollar Directory, The Thomas Register of American Manufacturers, The National Business Telephone Directory,* and *Ward's Business Directory.* You can use these directories to locate potential suppliers or corporate customers for your business.

If you need financial averages and industry ratios, look at publications such as *Robert Morris Associates' Annual Statement Studies, Industry Norms and Key Business Ratios,* and the *Value Line Investment Survey.* These guides offer key financial information for comparative purposes. I would also suggest that for any publicly owned business, you call and ask for a copy of the annual report. It contains detailed financial information on the firm and may offer other valuable information as well.

Hot Off the Press

The *Business Periodicals Index* lists recently published business articles by subject, company, or individual, and gives the publication name, date, and page numbers. The index is a great resource and is often available in computer, print, and microfilm formats. Just look up the topic in question and find out what is being written on the subject.

Many sources for statistics also exist. The *Statistical Abstract of the United States* gives population, business, agricultural, and manufacturing information that is current through the latest census. Other good resources include *Facts on File, Information Please Almanac, Survey of Current Business and World Almanac,* and *Book of Facts.*

The Encyclopedia of Associations is a three-volume set that lists all of the associations in the United States. It is a valuable source of industry and trade information.

Another source worth noting is a reference book entitled *Directories in Print.* This book lists more than 10,000 business and industry directories that give detailed information on virtually any subject.

Start-Up Help

If you are thinking of starting your own business, most libraries have several source books devoted to helping you get off to a fast start. Copies of *The Small Business Sourcebook* and *Business Information Sources* should be available at the reference desk. You may also find books on starting and operating a business in your state. There are hundreds of books providing detailed information on marketing, management, advertising, personal selling, accounting and record keeping, taxes, franchising, and other subjects.

Most libraries subscribe to a number of business magazines and papers. They can be a valuable way of staying current with trends and shifts within specific business areas.

There are three recommendations I would make to ensure that your quest for information is successful. First, know exactly what you are looking for when you start. Make a detailed list of the information you need and the form in which you need it. Second, use common sense. Look for natural sources for the required information and realize that you may not find answers to all your questions. Finally, if you can't find exactly what you are looking for, ask a librarian.

I love libraries, and I love librarians. The library is my secret source for answers and information. Now that you know about my source, why don't you make it your source too?

A License to Steal

When you start a new business, you are automatically granted a license to steal. Now hold on just a minute; I'm not suggesting that any business has a right to break any law or take advantage of consumers. The license to steal that I'm talking about is legal and doesn't amount to ripping off customers.

Actually, there are two "it's OK to steal" permits issued to every business. Understanding these permits and using them to build your sales is good business. In addition, using these licenses is legal, moral, and ethical.

Who granted these rights? Who issued these licenses in the first place? The founders of our country granted the rights and approved the system. They founded our nation as a democracy, based on the economic rules of capitalism and free enterprise. This system gives bright men and women a license to steal.

Grand Theft: Ideas

The authorities will not charge you with grand theft or larceny if you steal good ideas or concepts from others. Use some caution in this area. You may not use (steal) copyrighted material without permission. You cannot steal trademarks and service marks or items covered by patents.

However, no one can protect ideas and concepts. You have a license to steal good ideas and adapt them to your business operation. Concepts can be copied, modified, and used at will.

Some of America's greatest successes borrowed their success concepts from others. Dale Carnegie, the author of *How to Win Friends and Influence People,* admitted using his license to steal. Carnegie said, "The ideas I stand for are not mine. I borrowed some from Socrates. I swiped some from Chesterfield. I stole some from Jesus. And I put them in a book. If you don't like their ideas, whose would you use?"

Wal-Mart founder Sam Walton also used his license liberally. Sol Price, who founded the Price Club warehouse stores in 1976, said this about Mr. Sam: "He is notorious for looking at what everybody else does, taking the best of it, and then making it better."

Henry Ford also stole good ideas. Ford did not invent the assembly line concept, as many folks incorrectly believe. It had been used in other industries for many years. He just adapted the concept to making cars, and, of course, the rest is history.

So if you want to succeed, keep your eyes open. Look for good ideas that you can adapt to your situation. Determine how you can improve products or devise new methods to deliver services. Use your "ideas" license.

Purloining Customers

Yes, your license to steal also gives you the right to purloin customers. However, you do not have the right to take customers by force. Instead, you must steal them by appealing to their main motivations: the desire for value and the desire for personal respect.

Today's customers have better information and are less likely to be completely loyal to any business. Therefore, all business owners must stay focused on giving their customers good reasons and distinct benefits for doing business with them.

If you don't offer an advantage—value, service, convenience, variety, quality, ambience, product knowledge, etc.—you make it easy for others to steal your customers. Of course, it works both ways. Observe your competitors. Where are they weak? How can you serve their customers more effectively? When you find your competitors' weaknesses, you can steal their most valuable asset—their customers.

Writers also have a license to steal. I admit I stole this idea from a colleague. When I offered to give him credit for the idea he said, "Don't bother; I think I read it in a book somewhere!"

Goldilocks and the Three Barriers

If Goldilocks lived in our town today, she would probably be thinking of starting her own business. Millions of Americans are. Many of them are bright and inquisitive, just like Goldilocks.

I imagine Goldilocks would consider opening a trendy little restaurant. She might call it Goldie's Porridge Palace. Or perhaps she would open a furniture store. She might feature "just right" chairs and bedroom furniture.

One element is certain: Before long, Goldilocks would have an encounter with the three barriers. Nearly everyone who starts a business does.

Papa Barrier

The biggest, hairiest barrier is Shorty Cash, an alias for lack of money. Inadequate starting capital is probably the number one reason that many would-be entrepreneurs never get their businesses to a point of profitability.

Thirty years ago, it was not uncommon to start a business with a thousand dollars or less. Fifteen years ago, my wife and I started our first retail store with $25,000 of savings. It wasn't enough. Today it would take several times that amount. Many clients I have worked with have found themselves in financial trouble because they did not have enough money when they opened their business.

We encourage all start-up clients we serve to consider their initial need for money carefully. There are two kinds of costs to consider. First, there are the prestart costs. Rent and utility deposits, remodeling costs, inventory, fixtures, and promotion are all examples of preopening expenses.

The second type of costs is the operating expenses. Each month you will pay wages, rent, utilities, phone costs, and many other ongoing expenses. We recommend that you begin with a cash reserve equal to three to six months' operating expenses. If the business takes off rapidly, you may not need the reserve, and you can decide how to use the money to grow your business.

Mama Barrier

Another significant barrier to a successful business start is lack of experience. Operating a small business is often more complex than you imagine. We frequently work with excellent technicians who are perplexed by other aspects of running a business. For example, we might help a well-trained, highly skilled auto mechanic open his own shop. He knows how to repair cars, but he may not know about record keeping, financial management, payroll deductions, employee training, and workers' compensation. In addition, he may need help with marketing, advertising, and promotion.

He may be the most skilled mechanic in town, but he lacks experience in other areas. The best advice is to balance technical skills with other experience relevant to operating a business.

Baby Barrier

The third barrier is picking the wrong location. Baby, it can be a barrier. We made this mistake when we opened our first business. (Come to think of it, we tripped over the other two barriers as well.)

We purchased a "bargain" building just a block off the beaten path. We might as well have been out in the woods picking berries. We had to spend a lot of advertising money to offset the weak location.

Many entrepreneurs make their location decision on the basis of the cost of rent. Where the rent is lowest is where they locate. They may even buy the wrong building because the price is right.

Here are three basic questions to ask before you locate:

1. Is this location convenient for my customers?
2. Will this location allow us to grow the business?
3. Is this a cost-effective location?

The best way to overcome the three barriers is to create a carefully crafted plan for your business. To receive a free, one-page business plan guide, send a stamped, self-addressed envelope to: Solid Gold - Business Plan, P.O. Box 67, Amarillo, Texas 79105.

Know Yourself

Not everyone is cut out to be an entrepreneur. For a person considering starting a business, one of the toughest questions is, "Do I really have what it takes?"

Frequently, we are asked about personal characteristics that separate the winners from the also-rans. A lot of research has been done on this subject. However, the complexity of human personality and the hundreds of external factors that affect entrepreneurial success make it difficult to draw accurate conclusions.

Successful entrepreneurs can come from backgrounds of poverty or wealth, popularity or social rejection, broken homes or close family ties. They can be old or young, regular folks or real oddballs. Before starting a business, they may have been retired or unemployed, and ventured off in a direction entirely different from their previous career or experience.

Common Factors

One of the most common success traits of entrepreneurs is an intense desire to succeed. They want to win. They work long, hard hours and maintain a high level of energy throughout the long days. They start early and are self-starters. They are doers, not talkers. Even when they worked for someone else, they had a reputation for getting the job done.

This intensity is woven throughout every activity. They live and breathe their businesses. They are overachievers and are reluctant to accept defeat. *Perseverance* is another word often used to describe the typical entrepreneur.

Another common success trait seems to be restlessness. Entrepreneurs are frequently bored with repetitive tasks. They constantly seek new challenges. They love competition and seek activities that stimulate personal growth and development.

The easily bored entrepreneur should not be confused with the person who never finishes what he or she starts. The restless entrepreneur usually finishes a task, but will not be happy doing it again and again.

Communication is a characteristic that weighs heavily in the success factor scale. There is no substitute for the ability to express ideas and opinions well. This is true in the political and corporate world as well as in the small-business arena. Strong communication skills also include the ability to think and to listen. Many entrepreneurs become successful by listening to their customers. They utilize customer input to modify their business practices. These modifications bring them closer to their customers and place them in a better position to satisfy the customers' needs and wants.

In addition, most successful businesspeople have a strong self-image. They feel good about who they are. They like other people and tend to get along well with a variety of friends. They tend to be independent, but truly adaptable.

While possession of these characteristics is no guarantee of success, it can serve as an indicator. Any person considering the entrepreneurial challenge should carefully examine himself or herself. An honest evaluation of your personality, attitude, and motivation will guide you in the appropriate direction.

Buying a Business

"Buyer beware" is a phrase that was made popular by 1960s consumer advocates. "Buyer be aware" is better advice for the person considering the purchase of an existing business.

Over the years, we have counseled dozens of clients who made costly errors when buying a business. The following horror stories are true. We have changed the names to protect the identities of the individuals and businesses.

True Stories

Mark bought a small service business with his retirement savings. Even though the shop had been closed for a few months, the previous owner assured Mark that it could be a "going little business." Mark bought the building and the forty-year-old equipment at a price that was well above market value. He soon found that customers were not waiting to beat down the door. To keep the bills paid, Mark has taken a part-time job in addition to running the business. The stress of working two jobs is beginning to show. Mark is still a few months from being profitable and years away from recovering his investment.

Kim and Paul bought their business four years ago. They did not ask to see the books, and the previous owner was too busy to take inventory. They paid more than $100,000 for inventory that was worth possibly $30,000. They also bought an overpriced lease. Later, they moved the business, lowered overhead, and got rid of a lot of dead inventory. However, Kim and Paul have not been able to take any salaries from the business. Today, they would sell their business in a New York minute if they could recover their investment.

Rachel's three friends convinced her to buy into their business. Rachel bought the controlling interest at a ridiculously low price. Once her name was on the contract—and the notes payable—her friends pulled out. They left with assets that they swore were not part of the business purchase.

Fortunately, Rachel had enough money to replace the assets and should be able to weather the storm. However, it was a very costly lesson.

Ask the Right Questions

Perhaps the saddest thing about these three incidents is that they could have been avoided. Asking the right questions and insisting on appropriate information could have prevented these mistakes. There are five areas you should explore.

1. *Get the complete history of the business.* How long has it been open? Where was it started? Who started it? How old are the assets? Etc.

2. *Look at the books.* Any business worth buying should have a set of books. Examine the profit and loss statements, balance sheets, and cash-flow statements. Review the records for the last three years—longer if they are available. Look for trends in sales, profits, and expense percentages. Bring in a qualified consultant if you need help understanding the records.

3. *Examine the owner's income tax returns.* If the business's profit and loss statements vary significantly from the income reported, be cautious.

4. *Explore the owner's motivation for selling.* Ask a lot of questions and do a lot of listening.

5. *Evaluate the industry.* What competitors exist? Are they new? Is the industry growing or declining? How rapidly? What trends affect future business? Etc.

Once you have adequate information, it is easier to arrive at a realistic value for the business. While the final selling price is controlled by the seller, a knowledgeable buyer will be a better negotiator.

What Is a Fair Value?

Perhaps the hardest part of buying or selling a business is arriving at a value that is fair to both parties. The buyer must realize that the seller determines the initial asking price. However, knowing how to arrive at a fair price can put the buyer in a better position to negotiate both price and terms. If the seller's final price is well over the business's actual value, the smart buyer will walk away.

Either party may use various methods to arrive at a reasonable selling price. Most libraries carry books that cover these methods in detail. However, there is a quicker way.

You can use a two-step approach to calculate the value of a small business. The first step is to determine the current value of the company's assets. The second is to project future earnings and potential return on investment. This is more difficult to calculate, but the result may more acurrately reveal the business's honest value.

The two-step method uses the data you gather while doing the preliminary investigation of the business. Financial statements, company history, tax returns, and industry trends are analyzed during the evaluation process.

Under normal conditions, a business should be worth more than its assets. However, this is not always true.

One exception is a business that has low or nonexistent profits. Another is a situation in which the industry trend is declining. In such a case, the market value of the assets may be far greater than the profits would justify. To recover the capital invested in this case, you must sell the assets.

In the second step, be certain to estimate earnings conservatively. True earnings are what remains after an appropriate amount is deducted for the owner's salary. In a sole proprietorship, the net profit is the owner's salary. Therefore, you must reduce the net profit by the amount of a fair wage to reflect the true net earnings. For example, let us assume that a business shows a net profit of $20,000. If the owner can be employed easily in a job that pays $18,000 per year, then the true profit for this business is $2,000.

To find the fair market value, multiply the true net earnings (profit) by a factor of 3, 4, or 5. Use 3 for high-risk ventures or those whose history shows a decline, and 4 or 5 for solid businesses with strong track records. You also should consider whether the business is growing or declining. If a business is going downhill, consider the purchase with caution.

We have a handy guide that you can use to help determine the approximate value of a business. To receive a copy, send a stamped, self-addressed envelope to: Solid Gold - Value Guide, P.O. Box 67, Amarillo, Texas 79105.

The Name Game

A problem entrepreneurs often face when they decide to start a business is coming up with a good name. Every business needs one, but all too often we base our choices on emotion rather than careful planning.

Frequently, we see business names selected by ego: The Jane Doe Company or John Doe Manufacturing. It is also common to see business names based on a spouse's pet name, family initials, or coined words or acronyms that do nothing to promote the business.

Choosing your company name is an important decision. A bad name may confuse prospects, create a negative first impression, or keep potential customers from finding you at all. A good choice can boost sales, help develop a positive image, speed business growth, and make your business stand out from the competition.

You should consider several elements when choosing a name. First, will it be easy for your customers to remember? Second, does it tell potential customers what you do? Third, will this name help convey a positive image to your customers? Fourth, does it give you flexibility to grow without changing the name? Fifth, is anyone else using the name you've chosen? Perhaps a discussion of the most often selected types will help you.

Most Common Types

An often-used strategy for creating a business name is to use the owner's name. Eric Jones and Co., The Jack Owen Group, and Janice Doe and Associates are good examples. If you are well known and have an excellent reputation in your field, this type of name may work for you. However, it won't help if a potential client doesn't know you. In addition, it doesn't tell what your business does.

Perhaps the most common type of name is a combination of the owner's name and the business activity: Bob Day's Transmission Service, Carol's Custom Photography, or Francis Jones's Insurance. This type has the advantage of letting people know that you own the business and what products or services you provide. The major drawback is that it limits expansion into other areas without a name change.

Another type is a name that describes your company's primary activity or benefit to the customer. Some examples might include Letter Perfect Word Processing, Accuracy Bookkeeping Service, Quick Buck Check Cashing, and While You're Gone Pet Care. One benefit of this name type is that it gives a minicommercial for the business each time you use it. The main disadvantages are limited expansion opportunities and the possibility of conveying a negative image. For example, Quick Buck Check Cashing might imply that you are making a quick buck at the expense of your customers.

The final type is a purely fictional or made-up name: Nugen (New Generation) Corporation, The STAR Group (partners' four initials), and AAAAA Service (an attempt to be first in the phone book). This name type does give the user a lot of flexibility; however, it gives no clue to what the business actually does.

Keep your customers in mind when selecting your business name. Make it easy to remember and descriptive of what you do. Make certain it conveys a strong, positive image.

Just for Fun

Here are some business names you'll probably never see. I made them up just for fun. I hope you enjoy them.

House and Barnes—farm real estate agency
Hurt and Payne—dental practice
U. B. Owen—personal credit counselor
Rhodes, Street, and Bridges—highway construction company
Black, White, and Grey—ethics consultants
Ketchum, Cheatum, and Howe—attorneys
Slim, Chance, and Nunn—investment bankers
Leakey, Fawcett, and Pipes—plumbers
Adam, Uppe, and Downe—accounting firm
Posey, Flowers, and Moore—florists
Saddler and Buck—riding stables
Odom and Odom—bill collectors
Ogle and Snoop—private investigators
Dr. Ben Dover, P.C.—proctologist
Grinn and Barrett—oral surgeons
Shortz and Sparks—electricians

Home-Based Headaches

Starting a business in your home was the most popular start-up concept in the 1980s. It is currently estimated that nearly ten million Americans have a home-based business.

There are several advantages to starting a business in your home. These include lower capital requirements, convenience, and lower risks. However, many entrepreneurs who start at home fail despite the advantages.

We have counseled the owners of more than a hundred home-based businesses. We've seen firsthand the problems they encounter. Here are some of the most common errors.

Common Mistakes

1. *Leaping before you look.* The most common error we've seen owners make is jumping into business without thinking about the consequences.

Some owners expect to make a lot of money in a very short time. Many believe that business will come to them as soon as they open. Most don't have any idea how hard they will have to work to become successful. It looks so easy when you view someone else's success from the outside.

The solution for this problem is to create a plan before you decide to start the business. Writing a simple, but complete business plan will help you gather facts and eliminate mistakes.

2. *Leaving a great job to start a good business.* Some folks don't know when they are well off. I've watched several hard-headed souls walk away from a terrific job with outstanding benefits. Within months they begin to realize just how much they gave up for their independence.

A practical solution is to begin on a part-time basis. When the business grows enough to require all of your spare time and is generating a good income, then consider leaving your present job.

3. *Not having enough money.* This is probably the most frequent cause of early failures. To be certain you have enough money, put together a cash budget and income projections for the first three years of your business. Always include some extra money for unknowns. There is a Murphy's law regarding business starts. It says, "Whatever should cost a dollar, costs two."

Good planning is the best solution for this mistake also. Don't spend your hard-earned savings until you've thoroughly investigated the start-up costs.

4. *Underestimating your ignorance.* No one knows everything about running a business before he or she actually starts one. However, not knowing enough can be very costly.

You need not be an accountant, but you should know what records you must keep to satisfy the IRS. You need not be an attorney, but you should know if you can legally operate your business from your home. Many communities have strict zoning ordinances prohibiting home-based businesses.

You don't need to be an advertising executive, but you should know how to promote your business. Even if you have a better mousetrap, don't expect your customers to beat a path to your door.

5. *Lacking the self-discipline to work at home.* Motivating yourself to work at home is not easy. I often find many distractions when I work at home. It is easy for me to get sidetracked by maintenance work around the house, laundry, family, the swimming pool, and television. If you are going to be successful in a home-based business, you must treat it like any other work experience. When you go to the "office," you've gone to work.

You can avoid these common mistakes through good planning, a proper self-assessment, and a lot of self-discipline. If you prepare yourself and your working conditions carefully, you can be home-based and happy.

Chapter 5

Customers:
Your Boss, Your Future,
and Your Pot of Gold

The customer *is not always right,* and I can prove it. However, the customer is always the customer (unless you fire him or her), and that means that, right or wrong, customers are your future profits and your only job security.

This chapter is dedicated to the theory that the customer is in charge of the success or failure of every business venture. The customer determines who survives and who vanishes simply by spending dollars. Give customers exactly what they want, how and when they want it, and you're a winner. Fail to meet your customers' expectations, and you're history.

In this chapter you'll learn who the *boss* is, and how to deal with the four most common business myths. I'll teach you the three natural customer laws, and prove the long-term benefits of *good, fast,* and *cheap.*

Perhaps the most interesting concept in this section is that of culling customers. Yes, some customers should be *fired* or culled out of the herd. Not all cows have golden calves, and not all geese lay golden eggs. It follows that not all customers contribute to profits. I'll show you how to identify and cull unprofitable customers. It's good business and can add to your pot of gold.

Who's the Boss?

Ask a group of self-employed people why they chose to go into business for themselves, and you'll get a variety of answers. One common response is that the entrepreneur wanted to be his or her own boss. That brings us to the question of the day: Who is the boss in a small business?

Perhaps it would be appropriate to define the term *boss*. According to the dictionary, the boss is the main decision maker or the person with final authority.

In a small business with only one owner, who is the boss appears obvious. In businesses with several owners or employees, the answer is often less apparent. In large corporations, the boss is sometimes ignored entirely.

Therefore, it is interesting that the founder of one of the world's largest corporations never for a moment lost sight of who he worked for. Though he was listed as America's richest person, he knew who was boss. Because it is so appropriate to all businesses, we would like to share an essay written by the late Sam Walton. It is titled, "The Boss."

The Boss

There is only one boss, and whether a person shines shoes for a living or heads the biggest corporation in the world, the boss remains the same. It's the customer.

The customer is the person who pays everyone's salary and who decides whether a business is going to succeed or fail. And he doesn't care if a business has been around 100 years. The minute it starts treating him badly, he'll start to put it out of business.

The boss—the customer—has bought and will buy everything you have or will have. He's bought all your clothes, your home, your car. He pays your bills and for your children's education, and he pays in exact proportion to the way you treat him.

The man who works deep inside a big warehouse or in a retail store might think he is working for the company that writes his paycheck, but he's not. He's working for the person who buys the products offered in Wal-Mart's stores.

In fact, the customer can fire everybody in the company from the chairman on down, and he can do it simply by spending his money somewhere else.

Some of the largest companies that had flourishing businesses a few years ago are no longer in business. They couldn't or didn't satisfy the customer. They forgot who their real boss was.

The greatest measurement of our success is how well we please the customer, "our boss." Let's all support "aggressive hospitality" and have our customers leave 100 percent satisfied every day.

Get to Know the Boss

I highly recommend that you get to know your boss. The more you know about the customers you serve, the better you will be able to serve them.

If you work for someone else, this lesson still applies. Your job is dependent on company profits. Long-term profits come from satisfied customers.

If you work for a nonprofit organization, your job security is still dependent on serving your customers. With the possible exception of the federal government, funding for nonprofits is reduced if fewer services are rendered.

Get close to your customers and clients. Learn their needs and wants, but also go beyond that. Learn about their families, hobbies, backgrounds, and traditions. When you get close enough to your customers to be their friend, you may have a relationship that will last for life.

The only reason your business exists is to serve your boss, the customer. When every effort is expended to satisfy your customers, your odds of success are very, very favorable.

Four Business Myths

John F. Kennedy once said, "The great enemy of the truth is very often not the lie—deliberate, contrived and dishonest—but the myth—persistent, persuasive and unrealistic."

A myth, according to the dictionary, is a belief or story that is imaginary or fictitious. As I study business, I find that there are several myths that have survived for years.

The four myths that follow are persistent and persuasive, but not true. However, they do contain some truth. Perhaps that is why many business owners accept them as factual. The most believable lies are those that contain an element of truth.

1. *The customer is always right.* You will find this myth published in books, printed in articles, posted on signs, and even carved in stone. However, despite its widespread use, it remains a myth.

In this age of concern for service, we must try to guarantee customer satisfaction. However, we cannot hold to the extreme belief that the customer is always right. Customers are people. They are human beings, and like the rest of us they make mistakes. No customer is always right. For example, what if a customer came to your business and demanded to buy everything at less than your cost? Is the customer's price right? Can you afford to honor "the-customer-is-always-right" philosophy? Of course not.

In this example, the customer is unreasonable. The low-price request is neither right, fair, nor reasonable. The right price is not the customer's offer, but a price that covers your costs—including overhead—and gives you a profit.

2. *Customers always buy the lowest-priced items.* If this myth were true, you would see no happy Cadillac owners, no delighted Nordstrom shoppers, no satisfied customers at fancy restaurants, and no Rolex watch wearers.

This belief is a myth because the lowest price is not the only reason people make buying decisions. Price is an element of every purchase decision. However, value—the balance of price and quality—is the main determinant. Every business can enhance its perceived value by balancing prices with quality products, premium service, and consistent promotion.

3. *Discounters don't offer customer service.* This is still a popular belief among small-business owners. I hear this myth reiterated at most of the "Up Against the Wal-Marts" workshops I give.

I think the problem in this area stems from an incorrect definition of customer service. Many small-business owners and managers define customer service as a "friendly smile in every aisle."

Now I certainly don't discount the value of friendly, courteous personnel, but they are only a small portion of true customer service. Other important elements of real service are convenient business hours, clean rest rooms, trained telephone personnel, employees with product knowledge, product availability, attractive merchandising, consistent merchandise return policies, convenient location, cleanliness, and short checkout lines.

4. *Everyone is my target customer.* No business can serve all people effectively. Every business owner must learn to position the business to attract and serve a segment of consumers.

It is wrong to assume that everyone is your target customer. Even the megastores with acres of shopping area and tens of thousands of inventory items do not effectively serve all consumers. Some older, less agile customers are reluctant to trek down long aisles to find a few necessary items. Many senior citizens report that they prefer smaller stores with personal service.

Position your business to serve a strong market segment. Remember, those who try to please everyone often end up pleasing no one.

Three Natural Laws

Every day, natural laws affect our lives. Perhaps the best illustration of this is the natural law of gravity.

You may not know about or fully understand the law of gravity, but it's in force nonetheless. For example, if I throw a large bucket of cold water up in the air over your head, you will get wet. The natural law of gravity ensures that fact.

In business, there are many natural laws. Three of these laws have to do with customers. Armed with knowledge of the three customer laws, you might just build a better business.

1. *Customers always go where they get good value.* The dictionary defines value as "a fair . . . return for something exchanged." Customers will always do business where they feel they receive a good return (quality and quantity of products and services) for the exchange (usually money).

Customers are becoming more sophisticated in defining value. They spend more time finding the best quality at the most affordable price. Millions subscribe to consumer publications that guide them in selecting the best values.

High quality at low prices equals the best value. Nowhere in business is this point better illustrated than in the growth of the mass merchandisers. Wal-Mart's skyrocketing growth since 1982 is a primary example.

However, Wal-Mart doesn't own any customer. Customers are free to shop where they wish. If you can provide better value, the customer will come to you, because customers always go where they get good value.

2. *Customers always return to businesses where they are treated well.* Call it good service, great service, or outrageous service, the meaning is the same: Treat each customer as if he or she were the most important person on earth. Why? Because it's true. Research shows that nearly seven out of ten customers who stop doing business with you will have done so because of the way you treated them. While you may not have complete control of the value, you are in control of the service. There is no excuse for not treating your customers well.

Every person who walks through your front door is equally important. Whether dressed in overalls or a business suit, a silk dress or shorts and sandals, a customer is the only reason your business exists.

Good service begins with simple courtesy. A pleasant greeting with a smile is a good start. Call your customer by name, if you can. Then provide what the customer wants as quickly as possible. Remember to thank your customers sincerely so that they will know that you genuinely appreciate their business.

Definitions of customer service abound. However, the one I like best is simply "doing a little more than the customer expects." Remember: Customers always return to businesses where they are treated well.

3. *When the level of quality or service declines, the customer declines as well.* He or she declines to do business with you.

Some time ago, a business where I had been a steady customer allowed its service to slip below a level that was acceptable to me. I found a new business to fulfill my needs.

Surprisingly, I found that the new store provided not only a higher level of service but an excellent product as well. The clincher was the price. The new store charges 15 percent less than my former supplier.

Think about it. The new store provides an equivalent product with better service at a 15 percent discount. Where would you go? I'll stick with my new supplier because doing otherwise would be against the natural laws.

Cows, Customers, and Culls

For more than twenty years, independent businessman Bill Siebenborn has kept records. Production Unit no. 469 produced 28,000 pounds last year. Old no. 480 poured out 26,000 pounds, and no. 414 tipped the production scales at 24,000 pounds.

Siebenborn doesn't really enjoy record keeping, but he knows that without accurate records, he cannot improve overall production rates consistently. His records show that he has increased productivity by more than 58 percent since he began.

Siebenborn owns and operates a seventy-cow dairy farm in the rolling hills of north Missouri. He began milking on his own in 1974 after purchasing a herd that was producing well above the state average. Not satisfied with just being above average, Siebenborn has worked hard at surviving in a declining industry.

Constant Improvement

What is the key to Siebenborn's longevity? "Constant improvement," he said. "We have had to get better every year. We've used the DHIA's (Dairy Herd Improvement Association) record-keeping system since we began. It allows us to measure the productivity of every cow in our herd. We identify unprofitable producers and work them out of our operation."

As I thought about Siebenborn's success, it became apparent that we could apply the principles to all businesses. Success depends on constant improvement, good records, and culling out unprofitable business.

That is what management guru W. Edwards Deming taught the Japanese. He taught them to strive for improvement; to look for better ways to manufacture, market, and service each product; to increase quality and improve in some small way every day.

For Siebenborn, the improvement comes largely from culling his herd. Because of his very accurate record keeping, he can eliminate the unprofitable producers. They take a trip to the sale barn. He breeds the top producers to bulls with strong performance records in their descendent line. The result is new production units with positive genes that he hopes will become even better producers.

Culling Customers

Most businessmen and women would agree that it is good to have more business. Many folks interpret more business as more customers. However, having more customers doesn't always mean more profits. Some customers are unprofitable.

Just like a cow that produces well below the average for the herd, some customers aren't worth keeping. That may sound a little strange in a slow business economy, with most experts hammering away at keeping customers at any cost. However, I will stick by the opinion that some customers aren't worth the trouble.

Please allow me to make an analogy between cows and customers. Low-profit customers eat as much hay as top producers. Low-profit customers take as long to milk as any other. Low-profit customers require as much record keeping, management time, and used alfalfa removal as do your best customers. The message is simple: Every venture can benefit from culling out unprofitable business, particularly if you replace the culls with true cash cows.

In Siebenborn's dairy operation, all cows cost about the same to keep. This is probably true in your business. Most customers take about the same amount of care and feeding. So let's identify the good customers and send the others to our competitors.

I am aware that customer culling is a departure from the conventional wisdom that all customers are good customers. However, it is critical to recognize that not all cows are good cows and not all customers are good customers. With selective culling, you will have more time to spend on developing quality customers and providing good service to them.

The first step is to analyze your records to determine which customers are profitable. Try to find out what products or services each customer buys, what volume the customer purchases, and with what frequency.

Cull or Change

Careful analysis can identify customers who are robbing you of much-needed profit. For example, Joe is in the fuel delivery business. One of his steady customers is a retired farmer who lives twenty miles out of town. This farmer orders 100 gallons of fuel for delivery about every three months. He has been a customer for five years, and he always pays for the fuel on delivery. Joe feels that this is a good, steady account.

By analyzing his records, Joe knows that he averages 20 cents per gallon in gross profit on the fuel. The delivery truck costs about $1 per mile to operate, and it can deliver 500 gallons each trip. The driver's wages and benefits cost Joe about $10 per hour, and it takes one hour to make the delivery.

Each 100-gallon delivery earns Joe $20 in gross margin (20 cents times 100 gallons). However, his direct costs are $50 per delivery (40 miles times $1 per mile plus $10 for the driver). Should Joe keep this customer?

The records show that Joe is losing $30 on each delivery. That adds up to a total loss of $120 per year. It would appear that Joe should cull this customer. However, there may be a better way. Joe might offer the farmer a small discount to encourage him to purchase all 400 gallons at one time. One delivery would still cost $50, but the gross profit from a 400-gallon sale would be $80. If Joe offered a 2 cents per gallon discount, his annual profit would be $22 as opposed to a $120 loss.

Out of Balance

Ralph owns a small front-end alignment and repair shop. Business had been a little slow, so he offered a $10 wheel-balance special to attract new business. The $10 just covered his direct costs on a one-time balance.

The day after Ralph's newspaper ad ran, he began to receive calls and make appointments. That afternoon an elderly woman came by, and Ralph agreed to work her in.

Her tires were nearly new, and the balance was pretty good. He added one small weight and moved another slightly to make the balance perfect. He thanked her and sent her on her way.

Two days later the woman returned to complain about her wheel balance. Ralph checked each tire, and everything was still perfect. Together they road-tested the car, and the customer said, "feel that," "feel that," but Ralph could feel no vibration.

The customer came back the following day. The balance was still perfect, but the customer "felt something." Ralph decided enough was enough. He apologized for not fixing the problem and cheerfully refunded the customer's money. Ralph couldn't afford this customer.

The Time Thief

There are other types of customers who may be ripe for culling. One potential cull is the time thief. I'm convinced that a good many folks don't have enough to do. Or maybe they have plenty to do, but don't want to do it. Time is a precious commodity that is scarce in most businesses. Time thieves waste it as if there were a surplus.

As with the profit robbers, you may not have to cull the time thieves. However, you must deal with them quickly, firmly, and tactfully. Sometimes just pointing out how busy you are will do the trick. If your time waster is slow of wit, try a more direct approach. Say something like, "Bubba, I always enjoy visiting with you, but I've got to get busy." Then get up and get busy. Ninety-nine times out of one hundred the time waster will take your hint without hard feelings.

Another potential cull is the demander. Demanders expect special treatment. They want to go to the front of the line or move to the head of the waiting list. They expect you to drop everything and take care of them.

The following incident allegedly happened in the lost-luggage line at an airport back East. A very disgruntled passenger bypassed about a dozen people in line and went right up to the counter and demanded service. The obviously harried customer service representative tried to ignore the demander, who ranted and raved about his lost luggage.

Finally, she excused herself from the customer she was serving and addressed the demander by asking his name. "Brown," he shouted. "William F. Brown the third."

"Well, Mr. Brown," the service representative said sweetly, "right now just two people in the whole world give a darn about your luggage. And frankly, one of us is losing interest." He went back to the end of the line.

The Abuser

An abuser is a customer who can tear up a steel ball with a cotton swab. Several years ago, I sold a customer a high-quality weed trimmer. In a few hours he brought it back with the cutting head nearly destroyed. It had obviously been abused, but I installed a new head—no hassle, no charge—and sent him on his way.

The next day he was back with the new cutting head in the same shape. I told this customer that I didn't think this trimmer was heavy enough for his use. I refunded the purchase price and suggested that he check with a competitor to see if their brand would be more suitable. He had already cost me $30 in repairs, so why not let my competitor share the fun.

In summary, use your records and good judgment to analyze your customers. Cull out those who are costing you excess time and money. Spend the time and money you save to attract and take care of profitable business.

By the Hour

It's 5:30 P.M. If you fired a cannon down the middle of Main Street, you wouldn't have to worry about casualties. The same situation exists in most downtown shopping areas on Saturday and Sunday.

Why is this change in shopping patterns occurring? Why do most independent retail stores close at 5 or 5:30 P.M.? Why are so few open on Saturday? Why do so many small stores fail every year? Why are the national discount chain stores doing so well?

These questions were discussed, debated, and at least partially answered at a national meeting on retailing that I attended a few years ago. Some of the best research and hottest discussions were in the area of store hours and consumer shopping patterns.

When Do People Shop?

Richard L. Mistele, an associate professor at the University of Wisconsin, published a study in 1991 of hourly traffic at discount department stores. The purpose of the study was to see when people preferred to shop. Mistele's study proposed to answer three questions: What days are most popular for shopping? Which hours are busiest? What percentage of the weekday business is done after 5 P.M.?

The results are fascinating. Mistele's study reveals that Saturday is still the most preferred shopping day, followed closely by Sunday and Friday.

Hourly traffic counts were highest from 1 to 5 P.M. on Sunday and 11 A.M. to 4 P.M. on Saturday. However, perhaps the most interesting finding of Mistele's study is the weekday shopping pattern. More than 30 percent of the daily weekday traffic arrived after 5 P.M.

The implications are significant. By not being open on weekday evenings, local merchants may be losing up to one-third of the weekday business. By closing on Saturday and Sunday, they are forfeiting the two best shopping days of the week.

When Stores Are Open

As I considered Mistele's research, I began to wonder when the independent merchants were open. During a two-week period, I surveyed 506 businesses in five states. Here is what I found.

Incredibly, 239 (47.2 percent) of the stores did not have their hours posted. That's right, almost half of the merchants didn't even bother to let their customers know when they were open for business.

Of the stores surveyed, 194 (38.3 percent) closed by 5:30 P.M. Of these stores, about one-third were open only five days a week, one-third were open half a day on Saturday, and one-third were open all day Saturday. None of these stores were open on Sunday.

Only 23 (4.5 percent) of the merchants posted Sunday hours, and only 17 (3.4 percent) stayed open until 9 P.M. The remainder of the stores had varied hours but were open no more than five days per week.

If you are a small independent retailer who is trying to compete with the national discounters, let me offer some suggestions. First, consider your hours. Are you open when your potential customers want to shop? If you close at 5 or 5:30 P.M., you may be forcing your customers to shop at the discount stores. Remember that you are in business to serve your customers, not the other way around.

Next, let your customers know when you'll be there to serve them. Post your store hours and put them in your newspaper ads.

The price of growing your business is simply giving customers *what* they want, *when* they want it. The hours you are open for business are important. One way or another, we all get paid by the hour.

Good, Fast, and Cheap

Some time ago, I overheard a discussion between several small-business owners. They all agreed that their typical customer wanted everything to be good, fast, and cheap. However, they debated whether these three characteristics were compatible when combined.

The more I thought about that discussion, the more interested I became. These businessmen and women had put their collective finger on the heartbeat of the American free-enterprise system. We are all customers, and we want good-quality products and services. We all want and need affordable prices. We have come to expect fast service. We live in the "I want it, and I want it now for next to nothing" age.

Many companies that have recognized and exploited the good, fast, and cheap concept have prospered over the years. Ford Motor Company, Dell Computers, McDonald's, and Wal-Mart are excellent examples.

Tin Lizzies and Pony Cars

In 1908, Henry Ford introduced the Model T at $850. It was the first truly affordable automobile. In subsequent years, he produced more than 15 million Model Ts. Because of Ford's manufacturing genius, the "Tin Lizzies," as they were fondly called, eventually sold for as little as $260 each.

Almost sixty years later, Ford hit another automotive milestone with the "good, fast, and cheap" approach. This time, it was the Mustang, a brainstorm of marketing dynamo Lee Iacocca. First-year sales topped 400,000 units. The "pony cars" were an instant hit with the young and the young at heart. I was a senior in high school when the Mustang came out. I remember every detail of those little cars. Of course, I only thought about two things back then. One of them was cars; the other wasn't.

More recently, computers have taken the "good, fast, and cheap" spotlight. Personal computers now do in nanoseconds what took earlier models hours. Today's computers are incredibly small, fast, and powerful. I recently saw an ad for a brand-name computer (good) with Pentium technology (fast) for under $1,500 (cheap).

Defining Good, Fast, and Cheap

The word *good* has different meanings for different consumers. Over the years, retail merchandisers have diluted the idea of *good* by using good, better, and best quality differentiations. *Good* became fair or barely acceptable. According to the dictionary, *good* still means of a favorable character, suitable, and of intrinsic value. As consumers, we seldom buy the best of anything. We seek the best value, but seldom the very best product.

We look for dependability, reasonable quality, and consistency. I own a good American-made car. I bought it used and have driven it nearly 200,000 miles. It has proven dependable, cost-efficient, comfortable, and attractive. Most important, I expect to drive it a good while longer.

Fast is defined as easily accessible and readily available. McDonald's was a pioneer in the fast-food industry. It provides quick service, and the restaurants are conveniently located. Many Soviet citizens would be very happy if they could simply go into their stores and find any products to purchase. Product availability (fast) is a concept Americans take for granted.

Cheap also has different meanings to different folks. Advertising experts have substituted the words *inexpensive* and *low-priced* for cheap. This has given *cheap* a negative connotation. I like the word *cheap*. To me, it means affordability, good quality at the lowest possible price, and real value for the least exchange.

Good, fast, and cheap is a good concept for today's businesses. Call it quality, availability, and inexpensive if you like. However, good, fast, and cheap is what every customer wants.

Chapter 6

Planning:
Your Golden Gate to Success

It doesn't have to be formal, and it doesn't have to be long, but you'd better have a plan. That is the advice I give every start-up business owner I consult with. Planning is a high priority in most growing, thriving businesses.

In this chapter you'll learn the difference between strategic planning and operational planning. I'll tell you why planning is critical to your success, and show you how planning can help you cope with the unexpected.

You may want to start with a detailed analysis of your strengths, weaknesses, opportunities, and threats. This procedure is called a SWOT analysis, and it is used by some of the most successful companies in the world. I use this tool not only in my business, but in my personal life as well. It is simple, and it works.

The final part of this chapter is devoted to one of the most critical small business issues today: quality. I'll prove to you that 99 percent accuracy isn't enough, and I'll teach you the most important Japanese word you'll ever know.

You can plan for quality by creating a quality plan. Like the beautiful Golden Gate Bridge, a good plan can help you cross troubled waters.

The Survival Plan

Quickly. Tell me which of the following choices is the number one reason that businesses fail:

a. A bad economy
b. The bank won't extend credit
c. Too much competition
d. Lack of planning

The correct answer is **d.** Most young businesses—those that are under five years old—fail because adequate planning wasn't done before the business opened. Older businesses decline or go under because they do not have an ongoing plan.

Typically, the economy, the competition, or the banker gets the blame. However, objective examination usually reveals that the failure was the fault of the management. Even when the economy is slow, credit is tight, and the competition is tough, some businesses prosper.

How do businesses prosper in hard times? The management sticks to the plan. Successful managers always find time to plan. They change the plan to adapt to changing business conditions and stay on course.

The plans vary greatly because of the differences in the entrepreneurs. Some plans are done in a very formal fashion, whereas others are simple statements of goals and objectives. The common factor is not the type of plan or method of planning, but rather that there is a plan.

A Step in the Right Direction

If you don't know where you are going, you may end up somewhere you've already been. Even worse, you may end up someplace you don't want to go. Putting together a good plan is like taking a step in the right direction. It's just a start, but you're on your way.

A business plan will help you focus on where you want to go. It will also help you analyze where you are now. Once you know where you are and where you want to go, your plan will help you establish a clear-cut path.

For an existing business, the planning process should begin with a determination of your company's current position. Start with an analysis of your internal environment. What are your firm's strengths and weaknesses? What resources are available to you? Do you have reserves of cash and inventory? Can you identify areas where your company is unique?

Next, examine the external environment. Look at the local, regional, and national economies. Are they conducive to growth for your business? What trends are affecting your industry? How are your competitors reacting and performing? The main question becomes, "Does this environment offer opportunities or pose a threat to our existence?"

Once you know your strengths and weaknesses and have listed the opportunities and threats, you are ready to formulate your plan. Don't underemphasize the analysis part of planning. This becomes the foundation that you will build upon.

Two Types of Planning

Business owners and managers need to understand the basic differences between strategic planning and operational planning. The strategic plan concerns the big picture, whereas the operational plan spells out day-to-day activities.

The strategic plan details the company's mission and purpose. It answers philosophical questions such as, "Why does the business exist?" and "What are the general objectives?"

The operational plan finds the most efficient way of doing the tasks outlined by the strategic plan. This plan becomes the working plan. The company mission is broken down into definable and manageable operations. Company resources are allocated in the most efficient and productive manner.

Entrepreneurs are frequently guilty of being too busy to plan. The small amount of time they are able to devote to planning is used in operational planning. This can result in their doing the wrong things very well. Unfortunately, it doesn't matter how efficiently you produce manual typewriters if the world wants word processors.

Planning may be your best insurance of success. Although a good plan will not guarantee success, lack of planning will hasten failure.

The Winner's Edge

The world record holder in the 100-meter dash is only a few seconds faster than I am. However, he gets all the endorsements. The horse who takes the Triple Crown sometimes wins by only a nose. Yet, that horse will be worth millions more in breeding fees than the also-rans. The difference between a home run and a foul ball may be a matter of inches, but it can cost the ball game.

There are many parallels between sports and small business. In business, it is frequently minor differences that separate the winners from the also-rans. The price of your product or service may be only a few cents higher, but the business goes to your competitor. Another business may give only slightly better service, but you lose a loyal customer because of the difference.

There is an old maxim that says, "Don't sweat the small stuff." Don't believe it. In most businesses, you may become a statistic if you don't sweat the details.

Staying Sharp

Frank had been in business for seven years. Sales were lagging slightly behind previous years. Costs had risen steadily, and profits were lower than predicted. Although he had been earning a comfortable living, he had no reserve of funds to offset a bad year. Frank was getting nervous when he came to me for help.

A quick look at Frank's business practices and management did not reveal any major deficiencies. Overall, Frank appeared to be managing well. However, a detailed evaluation of the business began to bring some hidden deficiencies to the surface.

Frank had never closely monitored his financial statements. As a result of his inattention, several small cost categories had increased by large percentages. Individually, the dollar amounts were small, but when combined, they became significant. Because the individual expenses weren't large, no one had paid much attention.

Since the sales volume had declined slowly, Frank had not become concerned immediately. "This is just a slowdown in the economy," he had reasoned. "It will pick up again next year."

Frank didn't think he had lost any major customers. However, a check of the computerized client list indicated that several good customers had not made purchases recently. Frank hadn't missed them because he had been spending more time in his office with paperwork and less time working with customers.

Keeping the Edge

To ensure success, the best time to find and solve internal problems is when they are small. You must develop a knack for finding small weaknesses before they become too big to deal with effectively.

Weekly or monthly charts of your business trends may be a good start. Plotting business performance every week or month on a simple graph can give an early indication of a decline. Watch for changes in your gross margin, increases in expenses in relations to sales, and declines in net profits.

Another way to keep the edge is to stay in touch with all of your customers. Even small customers are important. Customers who do minimal volumes of business may offer excellent growth potential. Therefore, your attention to small accounts may pay big dividends later.

Monitoring cash-flow and accounts receivable are very important activities that many small businesses overlook. If you do credit business, you should monitor accounts receivable every month. A cash-flow statement should be produced along with the income statement for every accounting period. Monthly statements are fine for most small businesses.

As with the athlete who wins the race by a few hundredths of a second and the horse who wins by a nose, little things will keep your business in the winner's circle. The manager who keeps an eye open for small problems to solve will sharpen his or her winning edge.

Stuff Happens

Some time ago, I saw a sign in a retail store that made me smile. The sign was strategically located over a stack of environmentally correct diapers. It was adorned with a picture of a sweet little teddy bear, and it said simply POO-POO HAPPENS.

It brought to mind a bumper sticker I first saw on the back of a Texas cattle truck. The message was the same, but more crudely stated. If you've ever followed a loaded livestock transporter spreading the not-so-subtle odor of used alfalfa in its wake, you get the message.

Right about now, some of you are asking, "What does this have to do with my business?" That's a fair question, so let me try to explain. When you are in business, stuff happens. It is normal and natural, although not always pleasant.

In the real world, checks bounce, trains derail, suppliers don't ship, customers won't pay, equipment breaks, snow falls, and air conditioners fail. We may not like it, but stuff still happens.

How you react when stuff happens may have a significant impact on your physical and mental well-being. Most of the events that happen follow Murphy's law: Whatever can go wrong will go wrong. Here are a few tips on handling the unexpected.

Plan for the Unexpected

You should expect the unexpected. Good planners will always make provision for unexpected events. Many small businesses survive because the owners ask "what-if" questions.

What if our customers don't pay? Will we need to borrow money? Can we get a line of credit? How much cash should we hold in reserve?

Many small-business owners face cash-flow problems because they expect all customers to pay in full and on time. Anticipating "slow pay" in advance allows the owner to hold cash reserves or line up working capital.

What if suppliers don't ship? Are there other sources for the same products or inventory? Would these sources do business with us on short notice? Can we get our credit preapproved with them now?

Recently, we worked with a small manufacturer who had put together a strong business plan. The only weakness in his plan was that he had only one source of supply for critical components. He was betting the success of his business on the ability of one supplier to produce and deliver the needed parts on time.

Having an alternative source for components, cash, and credit is an important part of contingency planning. If you can anticipate what may happen, you can often solve a problem before it has a negative impact on your business.

Don't Overreact

I recently read a little prayer on the wall of a friend's office. It said, "Lord, help me change the things I can change, accept the things I can't change, and grant me the wisdom to know the difference."

When stuff happens, there will be some things we can't change. So stay calm and don't overreact. Ralph Waldo Emerson said, "Keep cool: It will all be one a hundred years hence." Ask yourself three questions:

1. Can I alter the outcome?
2. Will this crisis significantly change my life?
3. Will others be affected by the outcome?

If the answer to all three is no, then relax and go on about your business. Staying calm will benefit your blood pressure and stress level, and it will steady those around you.

Sir Winston Churchill told a story of an elderly man on his deathbed. The man reportedly said that he had had a lot of trouble in this life, most of which never happened. I do not want any of you to be troubled by what might happen. Don't worry, but do plan carefully and anticipate unlikely events. Then you will have a plan in place when stuff happens.

SWAT or SWOT

In law enforcement, when there is a crisis involving potential loss of life, the police often call in a SWAT team. These highly trained specialists know how to solve difficult problems. They are trained in the use of "special weapons and tactics." That is how they got the nickname of SWAT teams.

In business, we may also feel the need for special help. Unfortunately, there are few highly trained special forces to help us deal with our difficult problems. All too often, those who have the knowledge to assist us may be either unavailable or unaffordable.

While offers of free help may come from various sources, you should analyze both the source and the advice carefully. I know several business owners who have implemented significant strategies, only to find that the free advice was bad advice.

I've found that a good way to deal with life's day-to-day situations is to use some special weapons and tactics of your own. Instead of calling in a SWAT team, you can use a SWOT analysis. This consists of evaluating your own strengths, weaknesses, opportunities, and threats.

Do It Yourself

I find that we can usually choose a sound course of action if we analyze the situation correctly. A detailed analysis of our strengths, weaknesses, opportunities, and threats will provide us with many answers, and often will help us see alternative solutions.

To do a SWOT analysis, you'll need a pencil, a few clean sheets of paper, and a little time. I find that it helps to get away from other people and interruptions.

On four sheets of paper, I write, "Strengths," "Weaknesses," "Opportunities," and "Threats." I usually begin by listing my strengths in any given situation. The key to developing a useful analysis is to be completely honest. Do not be modest in listing your strengths. On the other hand, don't be reluctant to spell out your weaknesses. Honesty and thoroughness will give you a good basis for making decisions.

Some time ago, a client came to me with a real problem. A reputable company was offering him a contract to do some work. The contract was full of legalese that neither of us understood.

We did a SWOT analysis. We determined that my client was quite capable of doing the work. However, his weakness in the areas of understanding the contract and negotiating fair terms made him hesitant to sign. The solution was to bring in a professional negotiator who had considerable experience in contract work. The client spent a few hundred dollars to offset his weaknesses and earned a few thousand as he completed the contract.

Opportunities or Threats

Someone once said that every problem is just an opportunity in disguise. While I agree with that thought in principle, I know that businesses today face both opportunities and threats.

Opportunities provide chances to grow and prosper, chances to increase your business and customer base. Opportunities allow you to move into new areas and expand and diversify.

Threats, on the other hand, can take business away. Threats can take the form of increased competition, a slowing economy, or trends that would lessen the need for your product or service.

The best way to take advantage of an opportunity or to minimize a threat is to see it coming early. By taking an hour every few months to do a SWOT analysis, you improve your chances of being a business survivor.

Value of Training

If you work for someone else, training may be the difference between long-term employment and the unemployment line. Your job security is the sum of the skills you possess now and those you are learning.

If you work for yourself, training is even more important. It often means the difference between a failing business and a prosperous one.

Unfortunately, most of us spend so much time and effort minding our businesses that we miss many opportunities for personal and business growth. We devote long hours to our work and seldom set aside any time for training or for serious discussions with other business owners.

To grow and prosper in our businesses, we need to learn new ideas and techniques. If you are an employer, you should expose your employees to new information that will enhance their skills. Well-trained workers are more productive. They are more efficient and will help bring new solutions to business problems.

Corporate Examples

Many successful businesses are realizing the value of training. The Saturn division of General Motors, for example, requires employees to spend at least 5 percent of their work time in training or retraining. Not only do Saturn employees have the opportunity to build on-the-job skills, but they also receive training opportunities in personal growth and development.

IBM, although older and with more entrenched traditions than GM's Saturn division, also recognizes the value of training. IBM employees spend their first twelve months of employment in training programs. IBM provides about 75 percent of that training at its branch locations. Trainees spend the remainder of the first year in classrooms at IBM's national education centers.

At IBM, first-year recruits are highly motivated. They know what to expect from the training program, and they thrive on the intensity and competition. Although few IBM employees leave the company, those who do are often successful in businesses of their own. Billionaire H. Ross Perot is a well-known example.

Benefits of Training

There are many benefits of training. Some are obvious, while others are not so easy to discern.

From an employer's perspective, properly trained employees will help a business attract and keep customers.

Employees who are schooled in customer service and personal selling and who have product knowledge can help any firm grow and prosper. They add value to the customer's perception of the business.

In addition to increasing customer satisfaction and productivity, well-trained employees are more likely to become long-term employees. At IBM, first-year dropouts average less than 5 percent.

If you work for someone else, training will provide excellent job security. Employers are reluctant to cut loose well-trained people who do a great job consistently.

I would encourage every employee to seek training opportunities in three main areas: people skills, technology skills, and personal development. These skills will add to your employability and enhance your job satisfaction, too.

Training in people skills would include training in communication, grammar, writing, public speaking, personal selling, customer service, and win-win negotiation.

Good technology skills would include all computer-related skills, keyboarding, using telephone systems, and using audiovisual equipment.

The personal development area would include training in goal setting and motivation, business etiquette, health, stress and burnout issues, leadership, and time management.

Low-cost training is often available from high schools, colleges and universities, small-business development centers, and private-sector training companies.

Medium- and high-cost programs are also available. These courses frequently offer extended training in specialized areas. Check with your employer to see if the cost of any of these programs will be covered as part of your employment package.

Some final thoughts on training: You're never to old to learn new skills, ideas, and techniques. The more you know, the more you're worth.

We Need TQM PDQ

The operation of American businesses during the glory decades after World War II might aptly be compared to early freight traffic down the Mississippi River. Let's join a voyage of a raft, the USS *American Business,* as it travels from St. Louis to New Orleans.

The *American Business* is a large, well-made craft filled with American-made goods to sell when it reaches the Gulf port. The management team is settled comfortably at the front of the raft, pointing out sandbars and other potential snags. The well-paid crew is resting between shifts spent checking the cargo and manning the tiller.

The current is swift, progress is good, and the sun feels warm. It is business as usual, and everyone is enjoying the ride.

Suddenly, a raft filled with Japanese entrepreneurs passes swiftly on the left. This raft, too, is piled high with goods to sell. The only obvious difference is that every crew member aboard, including the management team, has an oar. Each is using his oar with power and precision to propel the raft quickly forward. Soon the Japanese raft grows small in the distance ahead.

The management team of the USS *American Business* exchange puzzled looks. "Wasn't that old Deming's management technique?" the president asks.

"Yes, that was Total Quality Management," the vice president replies.

"Didn't we try that once?" the president asks.

"Yes, but it made our arms hurt," the vice president says.

"Oh, yes, I remember now," the president says. "It made my back hurt, too."

Focusing on Quality

Fortunately, it didn't take American businesses very long to recognize the error of their ways. Not long after the Japanese sold their first "raft load" of goods, a few American firms began to take a long, hard look at W. Edwards Deming's quality techniques. Deming, an American professor, taught the Japanese about Total Quality Management.

Today, quality is the business community's most-used buzzword. Almost everyone is talking about it. However, many small-business owners believe that the TQM process is too complicated and the cost too high. Actually, TQM will save money. It is the cost of poor quality that we can't afford.

The High Cost of Low Quality

Most of us believe that if we did our work right 90 percent of the time, we would be successful. However, even 99 percent quality is not acceptable in many business situations.

For example, 99 percent quality would allow three mistakes or misspellings on every page of every book published to date. It would have us drinking unsafe water four days per year. It would cause us to be without phone service and electric power nearly fifteen minutes every day.

With 99 percent quality, every major airport in the United States would experience two fatal plane crashes each day. Fifty newborn babies would go home with the wrong parents, and doctors would perform five hundred incorrect surgeries daily.

Kind of scary thoughts, aren't they? Actually, 99 percent quality isn't a very high standard for business. We must aim higher. We must strive for perfection. We must set our sights on doing the job right every time. We must constantly strive for improvement.

The Japanese have a single word that describes their concept of the TQM process. The word is *kaizen* (ky'zen). *kaizen* means continuous improvement, involving everyone. The *kaizen* message is that not a day should go by in any business without some measurable improvement.

For Amarillo Hardware Company, the Japanese word has become as American as apple pie. This Texas-based hardware wholesaler implemented the *kaizen* method of improvement more than six years ago, shortly after Joe Wildman became president. As Wildman accepted the corporate reins, the eighty-three-year-old company was facing many new challenges. For example, in the 1960s, there were more than five hundred hardware wholesalers; today, there are fewer than two hundred.

"As we looked around our industry, we saw some of our competitors dropping out of business. We began to ask ourselves, 'why?'" Wildman said. "We knew if we were going to be successful where others were failing, we would have to improve."

Getting Everyone Involved

Wildman realized early on that improvement in any business function is dependent on the people involved in that area. With the help of a dedicated and talented management team, Wildman set up processes to measure, monitor, and improve quality.

"We learned early on that you can't improve anything you can't measure," Wildman said. So company personnel began by establishing benchmarks for quality.

The company posts daily *kaizen* projects on erasable boards in the employee lounge. Amarillo Hardware Company monitors financial progress, quality performance, and safety records on these boards. "Every company employee knows where we are every day," Wildman said. "We provide incentives based on how well we're doing. The better we perform, the greater the incentive." Employee incentives include cash bonus drawings, paid time off, and recognition at monthly Quality Committee meetings.

The Process Works

For the Amarillo Hardware Company, the process is working. Errors made in filling, packing, and shipping customer orders have been reduced to fewer than five per thousand order lines. Based on telephone follow-up, customer satisfaction is at an all-time high. The company is eliminating errors in its inventory verification process and reducing loss-of-time accidents.

"Whatever we measure improves," Wildman said. "Especially when we measure the right things, involve our people, and find the actual causes of quality failure."

Your future survival may depend on your adopting a TQM or *kaizen* quality improvement philosophy. If you wish to grow and prosper, measuring and improving quality is a valid concept. Even when you're headed downstream, it doesn't hurt to row.

Quality Tips

Some business-building concepts are so elegantly simple that we say to ourselves, "Why didn't I think of that?" This is the case with an Amarillo, Texas, company's quality improvement program.

Culligan Water Systems of Amarillo uses a straightforward approach for creating excellence from within. Tom Grimes, the company's owner, shared his five-element plan with me some time ago. The quality program was developed by the entire staff. I've read the five elements several times, and each time I'm reminded that good programs don't have to be complex.

Quality critics often criticize some of America's larger companies' TQM programs because of their complexity. The critics say that several of these programs are failing because the process is too complicated to understand and implement.

I realize that all business management issues are easier to discuss than to put into practice. However, if the process is too complex or if those who are responsible for implementing the program *feel* that it is too complicated, it is doomed from the start.

This is why keeping it simple and straightforward is beneficial. If you can express the main elements of your quality efforts simply, you can work out the methods of implementation and measurement.

Chrysler's Simple Turnaround

Lee Iacocca, the retired chairman of Chrysler Corporation, described his success in turning the troubled company around. He said the fundamentals were to "Create a quality product, deliver it to the marketplace, and make sure you let everyone know about it."

Iacocca's formula is neither complex nor difficult to understand. It is based on sound principles: Produce and deliver quality, and then promote your products.

To produce quality, many specific operations are required. You should examine each aspect of your business operation to ensure that it is contributing to quality in your products or services.

The elements of quality will vary from business to business. Some companies will be more product-oriented, others more service-focused.

The Q.T.I.P.S. Program

For Tom Grimes and his Culligan team, the quality effort began by identifying five areas to improve. They call their process the Q.T.I.P.S. Program. Here it is as Grimes shared it with us.

Q. *Quality.* Quality products, quality image, and (the most important factor:) quality people. Customers will pay more for real quality. Employees take pride in working for a quality company.

T. *Teamwork.* Work together toward common goals. Teamwork makes heavy loads lighter and laughter brighter. Insist on cooperation from all departments and staff. Eliminate bad apples from the barrel (your company).

I. *Integrity.* This is the foundation: honesty and fairness. Customers respond to integrity; employees thrive on it. There is no other way to do business.

P. *Profit.* Profit is not a dirty word. Profits mean good wages, new trucks, better products and services. Who is responsible for profit? Everyone in the company. Selling is essential for profit. Who sells? Everyone in the company.

S. *Service.* Service is the hallmark of good business. It separates the best from the rest. People take pride in providing good service. Customers demand it. The key elements are good people, trained well.

Start with quality and end with service. Build a team of dedicated individuals. Run the business with integrity. Watch the bottom-line profits.

Grimes summarizes the process by saying, "Q.T.I.P.S. sounds simple, but you and I know better. It takes dedicated people to make it work, and it is an ongoing process."

Part Two

Character Builders

The final six chapters of this book provide the guidance you'll need to develop a strong reputation for character and a record of achievement that will be admired by those around you. How can I make such a statement? Because I believe it. The truths, principles, and values I share with you have changed my life.

If you feel that success and happiness have just escaped your grasp, this part of the book is for you. It is also for you who want more balance in your life and career. And it will help you who have achieved a measure of success already, but are still looking for greater happiness and prosperity.

What you won't find is a "three-easy-steps, all-you-gotta-do-is, learn six-easy-habits, and leave-your-money-here" program for success. It doesn't exist.

What you will learn, as you read Chapters 7 through 12, are sound, commonsense principles for solving most of life's complex problems. These principles have been proven for hundreds—and in some cases thousands—of years. These principles work. They will change your life and catapult your career.

As you read each short segment, ask yourself these questions: How does this apply to me? How can I use this information to grow personally? How can I become a better spouse, boss, employee, friend, etc.? Remember, what you know can help you grow, but what you apply will satisfy. Don't just read it; make these truths work for you.

Chapter 7

Golden Role Models

I am who I am partly because of those around me. Some aspects of their lives, habits, and wisdom just rubbed off and became a part of me. Others, I chose to pattern myself after.

For example, I learned to smoke because a schoolmate smoked. I thought he was a man because he wore cowboy boots and smoked Pall Malls.

I learned to drive with my left arm hanging out of the window because race car driver Fireball Roberts often raced that way. I still would like to drive a NASCAR race car some day.

Other early role models included Stan Musial, Mickey Mantle, and Johnny Cash. I still know the words to *Folsom Prison Blues*, but I can't bat left-handed.

As I grow older, I'm developing an appreciation of others who, knowingly or not, played important roles in shaping my life. People like my mother, Helen Taylor; Abraham Lincoln; my wife, Sue Taylor; my eighth-grade teacher, Elgina McCracken; businessman Edison Raney; and my daughter, Christi Taylor. You'll read about some of these special folks in this chapter. I believe the examples and principles I share provide the foundation for a successful life. You can build a better future on these fundamentals.

The Ten Cannotments

I've long been a fan of President Lincoln. Perhaps it was because I was raised as a farm boy in the Midwest, as he was. Maybe it was because he loved to read and I love to read. Or it may have been because he was tall and thin, and I always wanted to be tall and thin. In any case, Lincoln was one of my history heroes.

In more recent years, as I have studied his life in detail, I have found two characteristics that I admire more than all others. The first is courage, and the second is common sense. Lincoln possessed large amounts of both of these two traits.

Lincoln was certainly a man of courage. It takes a great deal of courage to get up again after you've been knocked down. Lincoln was knocked down a lot. Early in his life, he failed in business, but he got back up. Later, he failed to win reelection as a politician, but he got back up. He lost a major election to the Senate, but he got up to run again. This time he was elected to the office of president of the United States.

His term as president also tested his courage. He took on the tough decisions and did what had to be done. He guided America through the Civil War years with a caring, but courageous hand.

Uncommon Sense

Perhaps what I've learned to appreciate most about Lincoln was his common sense. As I look around this great country of ours today, I see little evidence of common sense. Whatever happened to practical people who made sound decisions based on a study of reality? Did "horse sense" disappear with the coming of the automobile?

There certainly seems to be a shortage of practical wisdom. Common sense is so scarce that we might be more accurate if we called it uncommon sense.

Lincoln's wisdom and insight have been quoted by many writers. Some time ago, I ran across some of his simple, commonsense sayings that are worth sharing. Collectively, they are known as "Abe's Ten Cannotments."

I share them with you, with the hope that you will pass them along to others. Send a copy to a friend or family member. Mail a copy to your congressman or senator. You might even send a copy to our president.

Abe's Top Ten

1. You cannot bring about prosperity by discouraging thrift.
2. You cannot help small men by tearing down big men.
3. You cannot strengthen the weak by weakening the strong.
4. You cannot lift the wage earner by pulling down the wage payer.
5. You cannot help the poor man by destroying the rich.
6. You cannot keep out of trouble by spending more than your income.
7. You cannot further the brotherhood of man by inciting class hatred.
8. You cannot build character and courage by taking away man's initiative and independence.
9. You cannot establish security on borrowed money.
10. You cannot help men permanently by doing for them what they could and should do for themselves.

Don't you agree that these are wonderful truths? I believe we must profit from history whenever we can. We should focus on learning from those whose wisdom has passed the test of time.

Although Abe's Ten Cannotments are nearly 150 years old, they are still valid today. I encourage you to use them, share them, and take them to heart. Courage, common sense, and leadership will never be out of style.

On the Rocks

In springtime, nearly every valley in the Ozark Moun-
tains of south Missouri boasts a bubbling, gurgling little
creek. Every hundred yards of one of these nameless tribu-
taries is characterized by a dozen twists and turns, more
rocks than you can number, and pools of clear, pure water. A
few years ago, on a rocky ledge near one of these streams,
my six-year-old daughter, Christi, taught me a very valuable
lesson.

We were sitting in the warm spring sun with our chins
resting on our knees. "Daddy, why does the water run in the
bottom of the little creek?" she asked. Her question snapped
me out of my reverie. As a father, I've grown accustomed to
questions from out of the blue, and yet they still catch me off
guard sometimes. As I searched for a suitable answer, her little voice came again: "Why, Daddy?"

I tried to explain that water always seeks the lowest level
and follows the path of least resistance. To my surprise, she
accepted that answer without the usual, "But why is that,
Daddy?" We continued to watch the water ripple over the
rocks. I remember thinking that many people are like the
water, willing to follow the path of least resistance. They are
willing to drift along life's streambed with little care for what
might lie around the bend.

As I pondered this tidbit of wisdom, Christi stepped off
the rocky ledge and said, "Daddy, I don't want the water to
run over this big rock. I want to use it for a picnic table." I
patiently explained that the water wouldn't change course
because she wanted to play on one of the big rocks on the bottom. "But I want it to," she pouted. With her lower lip extended, she picked up a big rock and splashed it in the water.

Although I was vaguely aware that Christi was carrying
rocks and dropping them into the water, my mind returned to
other thoughts. As I struggled with business decisions, Christi
moved the creek.

Change the Channel

Well, she didn't move the creek exactly; she just changed the channel. Because she wanted to play on the big, flat rock, she built a dam that diverted the flow of water. Soon the sun dried the surface of the rock and her picnic table was ready. We enjoyed a wiener roast on "table rock" that very evening.

The lesson that Christi taught me that day is that we do not have to accept anything that we have the power to change. The rock she wanted to use as a table weighed several tons. We could not have moved it with a tractor. However, the water that made the rock unusable could be diverted. Christi simply changed the channel of the creek.

Don't Move the Rock

In our everyday lives, we all face problems—rocks too big to move. Instead of focusing on a problem, look for solutions. Orville and Wilbur Wright would never have flown by flapping their arms. However, they wanted to fly, so they built an airplane.

Henry Ford wanted to sell Ford cars to everyone in America. However, cars cost so much to build that not everyone could afford one. Ford changed the way cars were built, and made the Model T affordable for the common man.

Christi's lesson about the rocks has two points. First, don't concern yourself with what you cannot do; instead, concentrate on what you can do.

Second, you must persevere. Christi did not fully understand what she was doing when she started piling rocks to make her dam. But because she moved the rocks, the channel moved. She simply persevered until she got what she wanted.

A Strong Finish

Some of life's most meaningful lessons are taught to us when we are young. The only problem is that we often do not understand the significance of these lessons for many years. Such was the case more than thirty years ago at a high school track meet in Humphreys, Missouri.

It was a warm fall afternoon. I was stretching while I waited for the official to call the shot put event. One of our high school's best athletes was loosening up beside me. His name was Gary, and he loved to run.

Gary was a speedster. He had flirted with the magic ten-second mark in the 100-yard dash. Our team thought he would win that event, and we also expected him to win the 220-yard dash.

It was in the 220 race that this lesson began to unfold. From the beginning it was a two-man race. Gary got off to a slow start, but caught the leader at about the halfway point. I was watching closely and cheering loudly when Gary and the leader got their feet tangled up. Gary went sprawling, and his rival went on to victory.

The story could have ended right there. However, Gary got up and finished the race. He was dead last. Blood was streaming from cuts and abrasions on his hands, elbows, and knees, but he crossed the finish line.

As our coach patched him up, Gary gritted his teeth and vowed to win the 100-yard dash. Our coach looked surprised, but let him run. Gary won that race easily. He also anchored the winning 880-yard relay team and finished second in the long jump. Not a bad day for a guy who had resembled road kill before he was cleaned up.

The Loser's Limp

Gary could have developed the loser's limp. Certainly his injuries were enough to keep him out of action for the day. He had a good excuse to perform poorly, and every team member would have understood. However, he didn't, and therein lies the lesson: It isn't how you start, it's how strongly you finish that really counts.

Most of us start well. We get excited, set goals, make plans, and shoot off the starting line. Then we stumble. We may be seriously injured or just have our feelings hurt. From those real or imagined setbacks, we develop a bad case of loser's limp.

What we need in this world is a few more Garys. We need folks who will get back up and run again, despite the pain and anguish, and despite the disappointment of defeat.

Strong Finishers

History tells us of many men and women who were early failures, but strong finishers. President Lincoln failed in business and lost several important elections before his strongest finish—the presidential race of 1860.

Colonel Harlan Sanders, founder of the Kentucky Fried Chicken restaurant chain, was more than sixty years old and nearly broke when he started selling his world-famous recipe. He was a strong finisher.

Wilma Rudolph suffered from polio as a child. The disease left her with a crooked left leg and braces. She vowed to walk and run without them some day. And run she did. In Rome, in 1960, she became the first woman in history to win three gold medals in track and field in the Olympic Games. Wilma started with a limp, but finished strong.

The common threads found among strong finishers are the desire to win and the self-discipline to overcome setbacks. They don't quit. Like Gary, they get up and run again. Galatians 6:9 says "Let us not weary in well doing; for in due season we shall reap, if we faint not." Don't let life get you down. If you fall, get up and run again.

Jed Wrote the Book

Jed wasn't his real name. A teacher called him Jed, and the name stuck. Jed was only thirty when he took over as chief executive officer. He soon proved to be a clever businessman. He possessed wisdom beyond his years and pioneered many business concepts that are still used today.

Jed built a financial empire. His personal wealth was known around the world, and his fortune would rival those of *Fortune* magazine's entire top ten.

Jed was into mergers and joint venturing long before the Wall Street barons made them popular. He built and used the regional distribution center concept years before Sam Walton opened his first Wal-Mart. Jed was an expert negotiator and a sharp trader. Many companies still use his import/export concepts today.

Yes, Jed wrote the book, but it never made the business best-seller list. Most folks who have read his book don't even realize its business implications. However, if you find a copy today, reading it will help you and your business.

Jed Was a Planner

Jed believed in making careful plans. "Planning will put money in your pocket and quick decisions will speed you to the poorhouse," he wrote in one chapter.

There is no better way to prevent mistakes than through proper planning. Planning helps us determine where we are and guides us toward where we want to go. Planning allows us to map the steps to get from where we are to where we want to be. Like a good map, planning helps us establish direction, foresee obstacles, and estimate the resources needed to get us to our destination.

We live in an instant society. Nowhere is that more evident than among those who wish to start a business. We have counseled hundreds of individuals who can't wait to get going. They don't take time to plan, and that often leads to failure.

No Repeats

Jed was successful because he didn't repeat his mistakes. "When you make a mistake twice you're as foolish as a mongrel pup that goes back and licks up his own vomit," he wrote.

I hope you are not eating as you read this. However, the message is so important, I couldn't leave it out. Everyone who goes into business will make mistakes, but if you keep making the same mistakes twice, you probably won't survive.

Someone once wrote that success comes from experience and experience from making mistakes. Therefore, if you want to be successful, you must make mistakes.

Some of America's most successful companies have made big-time mistakes. However, they aren't afraid to try new things. If something works, they continue doing it. If it doesn't, they note the mistake and move on to other ideas.

Personal Worth

Jed said, "You can value a man by what others say about him." This principle is absolutely true for every business. The philosophy that you're only as good as your last sale is correct. It is also true that businesses are valued by what customers say about them.

What do your customers say about your business? Do they talk about your excellent quality, outstanding service, convenient hours, and great delivery? Or do they discuss the lack of these elements?

Oh, yes, I guess I should tell you a little more about Jed. Nathan the prophet—his teacher—christened him Jedidiah. He was more commonly known by his given name, Solomon. Jed is King Solomon, one of the world's wisest and richest men.

Jed wrote the book of Proverbs—the twentieth book of the Old Testament. The quotes are from Chapters 21, 26, and 27. I paraphrased slightly from the New International Version Bible.

It's Easier to Succeed

I received a new book in the mail some time ago. Since I love books, particularly those that offer a promise of help, I couldn't wait to read this one. Its title proclaimed, *It's Easier to Succeed Than to Fail.*

What kind of book would make that promise in the title? Can it actually be easier to succeed than fail? I wanted to read the rest of this story, and so I devoured the entire book the same day I picked it up at the post office.

It's Easier to Succeed Than to Fail was written by S. Truett Cathy, founder and chairman of the Chick-fil-A Company. Cathy is known in the fast-food industry as a man of faith and principle. The outlets in his nearly 650-unit chain are open every day of the week, except Sunday. That is part of the story.

How to Succeed

Cathy includes the following exchange in the introduction to the book:

> A highly successful person was asked, "How did you become successful?"
> He replied, "By making the right decisions."
> "How did you know which decisions to make?" was the next question.
> "By the experiences I've had."
> "How did you gain experience?"
> "By making bad decisions," he responded.

Over the years, I've observed the lives of many very successful people. They are not lucky, they are not perfect, and most will readily admit to making many mistakes. The difference I've found in the successes is that they always learn from their mistakes.

The winners learn from failure, grow because of disappointments, and, most of all, stay focused on success. They eventually win because they put into action what they learn.

The 74-year-old Cathy boils down his more than fifty years of business success into three key ingredients:

1. You have to want to succeed, and you must be willing to make sacrifices along the way.
2. You have to develop know-how. Cathy supports formal education as an important part of this process.
3. Finally, you have to do it. When you have learned your lessons, you have to put what you've learned into action.

Here are some other success tips from Cathy's book:

Other Thoughts

Shortcut to success: Profit from other people's mistakes and ask God to be involved in every decision that you make.

- To succeed, try this suggestion for success: Give 10 percent, save 10 percent, work 10 percent harder.
- Associate yourselves only with those people you can be proud of, whether they work for you or you work for them.
- Learn to love your work, and you'll never have to "work" again.
- Winners concentrate on winning. Losers concentrate on getting by.
- Ideas come from God. They are pleasant and exciting, but they won't keep. They have to be acted on.
- We make a living by what we get. But we make a life by what we give.
- It's always easier to dismiss a person than to train him. No great leader ever built a reputation on firing people.
- We never realize our greatest potential until we perform at our very best.

Perhaps the most important theme you'll find woven throughout the book is this one: We glorify God in our successes rather than our failures. My hope for each of you who are reading my book is that this year will bring wonderful success for you and your loved ones.

Persistence Pays

As a small boy, I watched a pile-driving machine at work. The operator pulled a huge weight to the top and turned it loose to come crashing down on the steel column. Though the impact shook the ground under my bare feet, the piling hardly moved at all. I soon tired of watching the machine make noise, but apparently accomplish little else.

It was not until some years later that I began to understand and appreciate the pile-driving process. Its results are cumulative. The piledriver must keep pounding away, even if it isn't making any visible progress. Persistence pays off in the long run.

For small businesses, persistence is one of the basic ingredients for prospering. Persistence is the continual striving toward the goal that ultimately guarantees your success. At times, you may feel that you aren't getting anywhere. When you feel this way, just remember the pile driver. Keep hammering away until you have built a firm foundation. It is steadfastness of purpose that drives many people to prosperity.

Plan the Work, Work the Plan

One way you can make continual progress is to stay focused on where you are going. Only when you have an achievable goal in sight can you measure your success.

I believe you should write your goals into a formal plan for your life. The planning process is a prerequisite for success. Plan the work, then work the plan.

The conquering of Mount Everest in 1953 is a good example of planning and persistence. Although only two men made the final assault on the summit, their success was the culmination of months of preparation. The project team included more than three hundred packers, climbers, and support personnel. They established supply bases at strategic points and stockpiled tons of supplies and equipment. Sir Edmund Hillary's team didn't just decide to go for a hike that day; they had a plan. Their success in reaching the top was a direct result of following the plan.

You will be more likely to reach the summit of personal and financial success if you first determine a course for your life. If you stay focused on that course, persistence will allow you to accomplish the most difficult objectives.

One More Round

"Gentleman Jim" Corbett was one of the toughest bare-fisted boxers ever to enter the ring. His personal motto, "fight one more round," became a tribute to his persistence. Corbett said,

> When your feet are so tired you have to shuffle back to the center of the ring—fight one more round. When your arms are so tired that you can hardly lift your hands to come on guard—fight one more round. When your nose is bleeding and your eyes are black and you are so tired you wish your opponent would crack you on the jaw and put you to sleep—fight one more round— remembering that the man who always fights one more round is never whipped.

Corbett practiced persistence. He won his first fight in the *twenty-eighth* round!

When life's problems drag you down and you feel like quitting, keep on trying. Think of the pile driver, Sir Edmund, and Gentleman Jim, and keep hammering away.

Take a moment and reflect on some of America's great examples of persistence. Remember Thomas Edison, who had hundreds of failures before he lighted up our lives. Remember Abraham Lincoln, who failed in business and lost several elections before becoming president of the United States. Remember Colonel Sanders, who was nearly penniless when he founded Kentucky Fried Chicken.

And, of course, don't forget Tommy Puttzer. "Who is he?" you ask. Tommy is the guy who tried only a couple of times, then gave up.

The Welding Shop

One of my early memories as a young farm boy is the wonder of Edison Raney's welding shop. I loved to go there and watch him work.

Mr. Raney's shop was located on the northwest corner of the square in Humphreys, Missouri. It served as a repair shop for farmers from miles around. When our machinery needed repair, we took it to Mr. Raney.

The shop was filled with interesting machines and tools. Later, I would know that they were welders, torches, grinders, drill presses, vices, and clamps. But until I watched Mr. Raney use them, I had no idea what most of the machines would accomplish.

Mr. Raney was a hardworking, honest businessman. He wore a funny little welder's cap that had no brim or bill. His work was hot and dirty. As each day progressed, his skin and clothing gradually took on the various hues of the greasy and grimy equipment he repaired. Even his face would change color as he wiped away the sweat of honest labor.

The most fascinating part of the shop was one wall where Mr. Raney had tacked up several signs, postcards, and articles. When we went to pick up completed repairs, I always read the items on that wall, if time permitted.

There were simple truisms like, "It is better to wear out than to rust out" and "The best way to kill time is work it to death." One little card always caught my attention. It was the story of a hot dog vendor. Though it's been nearly thirty years since I was last in Mr. Raney's shop, I can still remember most of it.

The Hot Dog Stand

A man lived by the side of the road and sold hot dogs. He was hard of hearing, so he had no radio. He had never learned to read, so he read no newspapers. But he sold good hot dogs.

He had a sign put on the highway, telling folks how good they were. He stood by the side of the road and cried, "Buy a hot dog, folks!" And people bought.

He increased his meat and bun orders, and he bought a bigger stove to take care of his trade. He asked his son to come home from college to help him. But then, something happened.

His son said, "Father, haven't you heard? The federal government just raised interest rates. The international situation is terrible, and the domestic situation is even worse." Whereupon the father thought, "Well, my son has been to college. He listens to the radio, reads the papers, and watches television—he ought to know."

So the father cut down his bun order, took down his advertising signs, and no longer bothered to stand by the highway to sell hot dogs. His hot dog sales fell almost overnight.

"You were right, son," the father said to the boy. "We are certainly in the middle of a great depression."

Proven Principles

We all are sometimes caught in the trap of the uninformed. We listen to others when we should continue on our

successful path. This often occurs when we listen to the educated, but uninformed.

Now don't get me wrong; only a fool ignores wise counsel. However, we must remember that not all counsel is wise.
Not all advice is good advice. Always temper the advice of
others with your own knowledge and experience. When in
doubt, get a second opinion.

In any small business, it is hard to better time-proven
principles. I'm referring to business principles like: Give your
customers good quality, treat them well, and promote your
business continually.

Thanks, Mr. Raney, for the hard work and good example.
Your business principles are still working for generations of
men and women today.

Chapter 8

A New Gold Standard

Prior to 1934, the gold standard specified the amount of gold of a certain weight and fineness that backed each U.S. dollar. The specification also covered gold made into coins in the United States. This standard was precise and easy to measure. Coins that didn't measure up were rejected.

Life has standards, too. We constantly measure our activity and productivity against some of these standards. These life measurements aren't as well defined as the gold standard was, and therefore, they are not as effective in letting us know how we measure up.

In addition, there are some who constantly try to lower the standards so that their own lives will be thought acceptable. They intentionally make issues murky and undefinable. They insist that there is no black or white, but only shades of grey.

Ignore those who would lower the standard and let me introduce you to a new gold standard for living. I'll prove to you that some standards never change or go out of style. Some issues are still black and white. If we lower our standards for living a quality life, we'll lower our standard of living.

In this chapter you'll find powerful words and principles for living a golden life. They're better than 10 karat or 14 karat—they're solid gold.

Three Powerful Words

Some time ago I had the pleasure of having lunch with an old friend. His career had taken a new direction since our last visit, and it was time to get caught up.

We had a good visit, swapped some old stories, and shared a few dreams. My friend, who asked that I identify him only as "Dangerous Don," then shared a few words of wisdom he had built his career upon.

I should point out that my friend is a nationally syndicated radio commentator who has achieved success as a professional speaker and humorist. You might call him the Will Rogers of the ninites.

Dangerous Don attributed his success to three powerful words. When I asked what those career-building words were, he replied, "And then some!"

He admitted that these words of wisdom might have been borrowed. However, it had happened so long ago that he couldn't remember who deserved the credit. I don't know whether Don was just being modest or if someone else really said it first. In any case, I knew immediately that I should share this wisdom with you.

Words to Live By

Those were his exact words: "and then some." Don went on to tell me the rest of the story. He said that when he was in school—shortly after the Dark Ages—he always did everything his teachers asked him to do . . . and then some. In college, he carefully prepared all his assignments, read the required materials . . . and then some.

When he got involved in sports, he did all the exercises, learned all the plays . . . and then some. When he started his first business, he gave his customers all the products and services they expected . . . and then some. Later, when he joined the professional speakers' tour, he worked to inform and entertain . . . and then some. Today, when he puts together his radio material, he works hard to entertain his listeners . . . and then some.

Then he smiled at me and said, "It's been a good life." In my mind I added the words "and then some."

And Then Some

Over the next few days, I found myself thinking of successful people. The words "and then some" seemed to fit every one of them. I thought about successful companies I'd done business with. I considered several that had gone the extra mile, provided special service, or done more than I had expected. The phrase "and then some" fit them, too.

Recently, I attended the funeral of an admired friend. As our pastor described this fine man's life, I found myself adding "and then some."

That is when it hit me. What our great nation really needs is a few more "and then some" people.

What if all parents devoted their lives to instilling honesty, virtue, and ethical values into their children? What if they worked hard to see that each child learned to read, write, and excel before he or she started school? That's what my mother did . . . and then some.

What if all teachers and professors not only shared the wisdom of the ages but taught by example as well? I was fortunate enough to have several educators who were positive role models . . . and then some.

What if the women and men we elected to serve us in the House and Senate became "and then some" folks? Then I realized that most already are. They spend our money . . . and then some. They raise our taxes . . . and then some. They take credit for all that's good . . . and then some. They deny any part of all that's wrong . . . and then some.

Alas, it just goes to show that you can have too much of a good thing. And then some.

An Attitude Adjustment

If you think you are beaten, you are,
If you think you dare not, you don't.
If you like to win, but you think you can't,
It is almost certain you won't.

If you think you'll lose, you're lost.
For out of the world we find,
Success begins with a fellow's will . . .
It's all in the state of mind.

—Author unknown

Since the late 1980s, I have worked with hundreds of troubled businesses. Some owners are able to weather the adversity and return to profitability, while others fail. One key difference I've observed is their attitude.

When the attitude is positive, there is hope. However, when the owner's attitude becomes negative, the end is near. Without an attitude adjustment, the business will fail.

By definition, attitude is the state of mind with which we approach a given situation. Our attitude dictates how we feel, how we look, and what we do. In business, our attitude establishes the way we deal with our customers and fellow workers, and even affects the tasks we attempt to accomplish.

Success Over Adversity

Doug Johnson, manager of the Office Furniture Outlet store in Amarillo, Texas, knows the value of keeping a good attitude. When a national discounter moved in less than a block away, Johnson could have been discouraged. Instead, he looked on the bright side. "They'll make us run a better store," he said of his new competitor. He added, "We'll have to work harder to please our customers." Johnson has worked harder, and the business is doing well. Attitude makes the difference.

Stan Greil agrees. Greil is the city manager in Del City, Oklahoma. He has observed the attitudes of entrepreneurs in several cities. "I deal with business and community leaders every day," says Greil. "Without a doubt, the ones with the most enthusiasm and the best attitudes are the most successful. A great attitude will take you to the top."

Attitude Is a Habit

Developing a positive attitude is not a one-time enlightenment. Attitude is a habit of thought. You can develop a positive attitude by focusing on the results you want. Then, your attitude will change to meet your expectations.

Good habits require time to develop. For example, establishing proper work habits may take several weeks. Begin by arriving at work on time and doing the most important tasks first. Take pride in everything you do. Even if no one else notices, you will receive great personal satisfaction from a job well done. Your attitude will change.

Respect and consideration for others also plays a key role in your on-the-job attitude. Make sure others get credit for their work. Pitch in and help whenever you can. What goes around comes around, and you may need help the next time.

Be enthusiastic, because enthusiasm fuels progress. It also fuels your attitude. Since attitude is a habit of thought, have enthusiastic thoughts. Ralph Waldo Emerson said, "Nothing great was ever achieved without enthusiasm."

It also takes a good attitude to overcome adversity. Dr. Robert Schuller said, "Tough times never last, but tough people do." Schuller was talking about an attitude adjustment when he made this world-famous statement. His words later became the title and topic of a best-selling book.

If you concentrate on developing the habit of positive thinking, then what Schuller says will work for you. When tough times come, you will have a reserve of willingness to tackle the problem and the faith to conquer the adversity. Your good attitude will carry you through.

Terrific With Four Ts

Over the years, I've met many pretty terrific people. Contrary to the headlines and the six-o'clock news, there are a lot of wonderful folks left in the world. You know the ones I mean. They are the folks whose names come up from time to time, and about whom someone always exclaims, "Oh, what a terrific person."

Have you ever wondered what makes terrific people so terrific? Why are they so esteemed among their peers? Why are they so often sought out for advice? Why is their assistance crucial to the success of so many worthwhile projects?

If you study the lives of these terrific folks, I believe, you'll find that four traits are always evident. I'd like to share them with you.

Terrific Traits

1. *The thorough trait.* According to my dictionary, *thorough* means "carried through to completion" or "painstakingly, especially with regard to details." Because so few of us ever carry out completely all the projects we start, thorough people appear terrific by contrast.

I'll admit that this is a characteristic I need to work on. Sometimes my follow-through is weak. I need to work on carrying out the details.

Let me point out quickly that I'm not advocating that you become a "detail nut" or a perfectionist. I have seen folks who accomplish little because they become obsessed with small, unimportant details. What I'm encouraging here is that we tackle a job and see it through to the end. If you become a stay-with-it person, folks will think you're terrific.

2. *The tactful trait.* Another characteristic of terrific folks is their tact. They have a way of expressing thoughts—even negative thoughts—in a manner that offends no one.

I used to think that some folks were born with tact and others totally without it. Now, I believe that the terrific person becomes tactful through studied practice. Terrific people carefully consider the feelings of others before blurting out the obvious. They are no less truthful than others, they just find ways to deliver the truth in less offensive ways.

3. *The truthful trait.* Ralph Waldo Emerson said, "Truth is the property of no individual, but is the treasure of all men." Terrific people share this treasure. They make it a daily part of their lives. As politically incorrect as it may be today, truthfulness is a terrific trait.

Telling the truth is often more difficult than changing facts to suit the situation. Truth is refreshing where lies are discouraging. Truth is freedom. Lies make you a slave to more lies.

Truth is tactful. The poet Robert Browning said, "So absolutely good is truth, truth never hurts." There are times when terrific people don't tell the truth. They don't lie either. When the truth would cause someone needless pain, they say nothing. They are no less honest for keeping some thoughts to themselves. In fact, that is one more reason they're terrific folks—they're thoughtful.

4. *The thoughtful trait.* Webster defines *thoughtful* as "considerate of others; kind." The terrific folks we know care about the feelings of others. They are courteous and polite. Before taking any action that might hurt someone else, they think. Because they think, they avoid many troublesome situations. Thinking before acting and speaking is an admirable trait.

However, there is more to thoughtfulness than being considerate of others. *Thoughtful* can also mean being careful and serious. The terrific person understands that you can solve some problems only with serious thought. You must carefully examine truth and facts. The person who can help you solve your problems through the wisdom of careful and objective consideration of facts is a valuable friend. In fact, Such a person is a terrific friend.

Old-Fashioned Ethics

Small-business owners enjoy a good reputation. People usually think of entrepreneurs as honest, hard-working, and ethical. My experience in working with hundreds of small businesses reinforces this reputation. In addition, I believe that business ethics play a vital role in small-business success.

Our free-enterprise system was founded on principles of conduct that have become blurred today. Insider trading scandals, the savings and loan industry boondoggle, and business and political graft have become the norm. The message is clear: Cheat if you have to, but win at any cost.

Maybe I'm old-fashioned, but I don't believe that cheaters are ever winners. One of the greatest joys that I derived from owning my own businesses was knowing that I built them honestly. However, following the principles of honesty and integrity is not always easy.

Ethical Dilemmas

The following incidents are true-life examples that businesspeople have shared with us. The names and genders have been changed for reasons of confidentiality.

Joe had an opportunity to hire his competitor's area manager. The manager promised to bring Joe the competitor's customer lists, pricing policy, and sales records. This information would help Joe's struggling business. Should he hire the manager?

Frequently, Mary is paid in cash for her work. Her business is not very profitable, and she wonders if it would be OK to spend the cash and not report the revenue. Mary's friends have told her that the Internal Revenue Service is corrupt and already collects too much tax money. Should Mary report the cash?

Bill closed a big loan at the bank. A few days after the papers were signed, he noticed a large error. The bank had inadvertently omitted the largest piece of equipment used to collateralize the loan. Should Bill point out the error?

A Three-Point Check

The answer to many ethical questions can be found in *The Power of Ethical Management,* by Kenneth Blanchard and Norman Vincent Peale. They suggest using a three-question test to determine what is ethical behavior:

1. Is it legal?
2. Is it fair to all?
3. Would I be happy if the whole story were made public?

These three questions make any issue that involves questionable ethics easier to tackle. The legal question establishes a minimum criterion. If it is against the law, don't get involved. The fairness question asks if it would be OK if I were on the receiving end of the deal. The third question asks if it would be all right if the whole story were printed on the front page of the local newspaper.

Using this method, the ethical dilemmas faced by Joe, Mary, and Bill become fairly simple decisions. While it is legal for Joe to hire the manager, the manager's proposal is not fair to all parties. The information that the manager is offering to bring to Joe's company will give Joe an unfair advantage. Joe wouldn't want the situation reversed or made public knowledge.

Mary's dilemma is answered by the first question. Not reporting cash income is tax evasion, a punishable crime. Even though we may not like the IRS, the law says that we must pay taxes on all income.

Bill's situation may not involve legality. However, the question of fairness certainly is relevant. It will not be fair to the bank if the error is not reported. Bill can solidify his good working relationship with the bank by pointing out the irregularity.

Many of life's toughest problems can be solved by asking the ethics test questions: Is it legal? Is it fair? Would I want everyone to know about it? One of the best comments I've heard on the subject of ethics is that there is no right way to do a wrong thing.

Follow Through

John and Mary had a great idea for a new business. They attended a "How to Start Your Own Business" seminar and got advice from their CPA and their attorney. Six months later, they were still just talking about their great idea. Why? They didn't follow through.

Bill's company was struggling. He brought in a consultant to survey the problems. The consultant examined the financial statements, reviewed the marketing plan, and interviewed key employees. He then recommended specific actions. The advice was sound, and Bill agreed. The consultant left, but Bill did not implement any of the recommendations. Six months later, the company went under. Why? Bill didn't follow through.

The committee chairman defined the problem. Committee members suggested possible solutions. After discussion, they approved a course of action and moved on to other business. The following year, a new committee was appointed, but the original problem still existed. Why? No one followed through.

From time to time, most of us are guilty of not following through. Our intentions are good and we're excited about the project, but we never see it through to completion.

Four Key Elements

First, to ensure complete follow-through, you have to make a commitment. You must be determined to complete the project, solve the problem, or make the change.

It may be necessary to put your commitment in writing. Small-business owners talk about planning, but few have written business plans. Many people talk about their dreams and aspirations, but few write them down. When you put it in writing, you are more likely to follow through.

The second key is setting a timeframe. A common cause of procrastination is not establishing specific time commitments.

This book might still be sitting on my desk if I didn't have a deadline. Publishers have a timeframe. Each manuscript must arrive well in advance of the date of publication. The deadline forces writers to complete their work on schedule.

Try it on your next problem or project. Give yourself a clear, definite date for completion. Make that timeframe a part of your commitment.

The third key is to avoid getting sidetracked. Most of us are busy and have many projects to complete. However, good follow-through demands that you stay focused on the objective. Consider eliminating any competing projects.

If you are like me, you find it hard to say no. From time to time, I discover I've taken on too many activities. When I become overcommitted all of my work suffers.

That brings us to the fourth essential element for good follow-through: Do a few things well. It is much easier to complete what you start when you have only a few tasks to do. Time and time again, I've seen organizations, businesses, and individuals try to be everything to everyone. It just doesn't work.

The best-run companies stick with what they know. They concentrate on being the very best in their niche or field. They concern themselves with only a few issues, but they perform those tasks to perfection.

Practice What You Preach

When my wife reads this book, she will suggest that I practice what I preach. She will point out the partially completed projects around our house. She may suggest that I make a commitment to finish some of them. She may even ask me to put the deadline in writing. It just might work, if I don't find another project to start first.

Increasing Our Value

Last year's baseball strike caused me to start thinking about what our labor is actually worth. As I pondered the salary of a $5-million-per-year baseball star, I began to calculate just how much that really is.

For example, a $5 million player who plays every game will earn more than $30,000 per day. That's good money if you can get it.

Some of us who earn considerably less might be quick to judge these salaries as excessive. The point of this thought is not to condemn those who have great earning power. I'm glad they have it, and I'm not jealous of it. (Well, maybe I'm just a little jealous.)

When you look at the big picture, how much we earn is only a partial indicator of our value to others. There are folks at the bottom of the wage scale who are grossly overpaid. Some minimum-wage earners are worth less proportionately than million-dollar ballplayers.

The focus and thrust of this thought is to help us make sure we don't fall into the "worth less than we're paid" category. My personal goals are to be worth more than I'm paid, and to be paid very well.

I've found in examining the lives of successful people that they all work hard to increase their value to others, ultimately increasing the amount they are paid. Here are a few of their secrets:

Add Value to Your Work

- *Become a "go-to" person.* In sports there is usually a player whom the manager or coach wants in control of critical situations. In baseball, it's a hard-throwing relief pitcher or a clutch hitter who can get on base. In basketball, it's the person you want to take the last shot. In football, it's the running back who will always get the two yards needed or the receiver who can stay inbounds and pick up the first down.

You can increase your value by building a reputation for getting the job done. Become your organization's *go-to* person. Concentrate on accomplishing the work, not on finding reasons why it can't be done.

- *Say "I don't know" if you don't know.* However, never say "I don't know" without following up with, "but I'll find out."

When you have the answers, you can help solve the problem. More important you'll acquire additional knowledge, and knowledge will increase your value to others.

- *Value other people's time.* Don't call unnecessary meetings. Be on time for appointments. Don't waste an associate's time by discussing last night's television reruns. Work hard to keep all discussions on track.

- *Look for work that needs to be done.* Most jobs have some slow times. Instead of coasting, use these opportunities to increase your value.

When you see something that needs doing, write yourself a reminder note if you don't have time to do it then. When a slow time comes, you'll have something to do. This is a great way to increase your job security.

- *Capitalize on your mistakes.* If you do anything at all, you will make mistakes. However, remember that mistakes are the building blocks of experience, and experience is the foundation of success.

Therefore, don't focus on the mistakes you've made. Instead, learn from them, harness their power, and use the experience to increase your value. Mistakes can teach you what you need to learn.

- *Keep your integrity.* Honesty is still the only policy. Your personal value is not tied to the integrity of our nation's leaders. Our superiors will judge us on our own merits.

You'll never lose value by being honest. You'll find that honesty builds trust, and trust adds value and satisfaction.

Try a Little TLC

To most people, the initials TLC stand for tender loving care. I believe in tender loving care, but in this book, TLC represents trust, loyalty, and commitment.

These three personal characteristics will help assure your success in life. Whether you own your own business or work for someone else, being trustworthy, loyal, and committed is important.

Trust

As an entrepreneur, I was fortunate enough to surround myself with trustworthy people on whom I could depend. These employees worked as hard when I was on vacation as when I was standing right beside them. Day after day, they earned my trust.

Trust is a funny thing. You would not keep an employee around whom you could not trust. However, there are many levels of trust. You may trust some employees more than others.

For example, you trust most employees with company funds. For many businesses, this is not a problem. Company time is an entirely different matter. Many employees who would never take a penny from the cash register think nothing of coming in a few minutes late every morning. They embezzle a few minutes during the noon hour and leave early if the boss is out of town.

These petty infractions can add up to hundreds or thousands of dollars in lost time. They also eat away at the level of trust. You may have to terminate the most skilled and qualified employee if the level of trust continues to deteriorate.

Loyalty

Loyalty is another form of trust. A. P. Gouthey said, "Loyalty is the one thing a leader cannot do without." True loyalty goes beyond blind love or admiration. Loyal employees will most likely know the faults and weaknesses of the boss and the company. However, they will strive for success in spite of those weaknesses.

Loyal employees will work hard to maintain the right direction when things are going well. When things are going poorly, you can count on them to pitch in and help right the wrongs.

If you are in business, one of your most important assets is a loyal customer base. At the very best, customer loyalty is fragile. Loyalty bonds are difficult to establish, but easily broken.

You must earn customer loyalty. Customers stay loyal only to businesses that provide consistent quality in their products and services. Remember the two natural laws regarding customers:

1. Customers always go where they receive good value.
2. Customers always return when you treat them well.

Commitment

Most successes in life require commitment. One trait of commitment is honoring your word. Keeping your verbal commitments will go far in impressing your customers, employees, and bosses. If you promise to get something done, do it. If you agree to meet at a certain time and place, be there. If you pledge your support to a project, follow through.

Committed employees will consistently do more than they are paid to do. If you are an employee who agreed to work for $5 per hour, start doing $7 worth of work. It won't take your boss long to notice you and what you are accomplishing. You may not receive a pay raise immediately. However, you will have the personal satisfaction of knowing that you are worth more than you are earning.

Commitment also means hanging in there during the tough times. It's easy to be a team player when the team is winning. It's another matter when the going gets tough. Only those team players who are committed will last through the difficult times. You could say that when the going gets tough, the committed keep going.

Trust, loyalty, and commitment are the winner's version of TLC. I hope these traits will become your new goals for personal and business growth.

The Power of Optimism

Franklin D. Roosevelt once said, "The only limit to our realization of tomorrow will be our doubts of today."

During the Great Depression, the president of the Los Angeles Chamber of Commerce was quizzed about the effects of the depression in Los Angeles. He replied, "Depression? We have no depression in Los Angeles, but I will admit that we are having the worst boom in many, many years." This community leader was a classic example of optimism.

According to Webster's dictionary, an optimist is a person who looks at actions and events and anticipates the best possible outcomes. Many humorous definitions of optimism exist— for example, a person who takes a frying pan on a fishing trip or a lottery ticket buyer who first opens a savings account. My favorite is the man who falls from an airplane without a parachute and as he hurtles toward the earth remarks, "What a beautiful view."

In the more serious world of small business, optimism is valuable. If a pessimist ever opened a successful business, I haven't heard about it. Nearly all new ventures are started by optimistic folks who believe that the outcome will be successful. I'll admit that I've seen a few who were foolishly optimistic, but there would be no successes if no one tried.

A Driving Force

Optimism is a motivator. The belief that something good is going to happen because of our efforts gets us up and going. Optimism is a driving force that helps us make the best of a bad situation. It is a state of mind that keeps our expectations high. When failure looms just ahead, the optimist will keep on going because of the basic belief that success is just around the corner.

An interesting phenomenon occurs with optimistic people: Good things happen to them. Optimism is the fuel of a positive attitude that powers people toward success. In a wide variety of careers, you will find that people who have great attitudes will soar to the top. Best-selling author and professional motivator Zig Ziglar said, "Your attitude determines your altitude."

Everyone enjoys being around winners. Just watch the fans at sporting events. Watch the crowds gather around successful folks from all walks of life. One of the common factors you will find in the lives of successful people is a positive attitude.

Some time ago I spoke to the members of a Texas Optimist Club. After the meeting, one of the club members gave me a copy of the Optimist Creed. The creed is a collection of positive thoughts that will help you build a positive, optimistic attitude.

Would you like to develop a better attitude? Would you like to be more successful? Would you like to enjoy a happier, more fulfilling life? Try following the Optimist Creed.

The Optimist Creed

Promise yourself—
To be so strong that nothing can disturb your peace
of mind.
To talk health, happiness, and prosperity to every
person you meet.
To make all your friends feel that there is something
in them.
To look at the sunny side of everything and make
your optimism come true.
To think only of the best, to work only for the best,
and expect only the best.
To be just as enthusiastic about the success of others
as you are about your own.

To forget the mistakes of the past and press on to the greater achievements of the future.

To wear a cheerful countenance at all times and give every living creature you meet a smile.

To give so much time to the improvement of yourself that you have no time to criticize others.

To be too large to worry, too noble for anger, too strong for fear, and too happy to permit the presence of trouble.

Chapter 9

Spinning Skills Into Gold

An auto mechanic friend of mine once told me that he charged $100 for a specific repair. When I questioned the price, he said he got $10 for doing the work and $90 for knowing how. And so it is with many things in life. We're often paid more for knowing than for doing.

In this chapter you'll learn some *must knows* for increasing your earning power. I'll show you that you can accomplish more by working smart than by working hard. And, that the combination of smart work and hard work is unbeatable.

You'll learn how to tell distant dreams from doable deals, and how to use the law of increasing returns to increase your value to others. I'll share some key points for building your communication skills and networking.

This chapter will help you know the steps required to climb the ladder of success. In addition, it will guide you through the process one rung at a time.

Skills are acquired through knowledge and practice. There is no easy way, and there are few bona fide shortcuts. So read on. There is no better time than right now for spinning skills into gold.

Working Smart

According to Franklin P. Jones, "Most people like hard work. Particularly when they are paying for it."

Ah, the virtues of hard work. Nearly every "self-made" person will tell you that his or her success is the result of hard work. Now don't get me wrong, I enjoy watching hard work as much as the next person. However, hard work alone is no guarantee of success. Perhaps the following story will illustrate my point.

Two lumberjacks were assigned the task of cutting down a stand of pines. Frank was a big, burly man who swung an axe with the best. Peter was small and new to the logging crew.

The two men started at opposite ends of the grove, and soon Frank downed his first tree. He was a little surprised when Peter's first tree fell shortly after his own. For an hour the two men downed trees at a nearly equal rate.

Frank continued chopping steadily and smiled to himself as he saw Peter stop to rest. However, Peter soon resumed chopping, and Frank was surprised when the two trees crashed to the ground at nearly the same time.

Frank redoubled his efforts. Chips flew as his axe bit deep into the soft wood. However, by lunchtime Peter had cut down more trees even though he had taken several short breaks.

Frank vowed to catch up. Right after lunch he renewed the assault with vigor. He chopped relentlessly, but he still lost ground. By the end of the day, Peter had cut seven more trees than Frank. As they rode the wagon back to the logging camp at dusk, Frank asked Peter how he cut down more trees and still took so many rest breaks. Peter looked surprised. "I wasn't just resting," he said. "I was sharpening my axe."

It's Not How Hard You Work

In the past eight years, I've consulted with more than 1,500 entrepreneurs. I'm learning that success depends not only on how hard you chop, but also on how often you sharpen your axe. To say it another way, it isn't how hard you work, but how smart you work.

Working smarter is not natural for most entrepreneurs. They are doers by nature. They have strong personalities, and they make things happen. When they get behind, their natural tendency is to chop harder. However, it is only when this natural tendency is combined with the skill of working smarter that the productivity level increases significantly.

The PIE Theory

There are three critical elements of working smarter. The first letters of these elements form the acronym PIE.

The P stands for *planning*. Thousands of years ago the great King Solomon penned these words: "The plans of the diligent lead surely to profit" (Proverbs 21:5, NIV). The more I work with small businesses, the more I believe the wisdom of this passage. Planning is surely the "axe sharpening" of business.

The I in the PIE theory is *implementation*. Even the very best of plans need to be put into action. There is work involved. Planning keeps the axe sharp, and implemenation swings the axe.

A common mistake in implementation is failing to take time to do the right job right the first time. Those who rush at life as if they were killing snakes frequently miss the mark. However, they always find time to do the job correctly the second time.

The third element in the PIE theory is *evaluation*. Plans must include goals that we can measure to determine their effectiveness. For example, our plan might call for reducing defects to one part per million produced. We can measure production results to see if we met our goal.

Plan, implement, and evaluate: the sequence of working smarter, not harder. Perhaps Ogden Nash summed it up best with these words, "If you don't want to work, you have to work to earn enough money so that you won't have to work."

Dreams With Deadlines

I've never traveled the highway that connects the continental United States with Alaska, but I will one day. I've never written a best-selling book, but I will one day. I've never walked on a street of gold, but I will one day. How do I know that I will accomplish these dreams? Because they are more than dreams; they are my goals.

Best-selling author Harvey MacKay said that goals are just dreams with deadlines. Most of the people I've met don't have goals, they just have dreams. Dreams that aren't well defined and have no timeframes are just dreams. Goals establish deadlines and give us focus. Focus means having a clear picture of your subject. People who set goals develop sharp, long-term focus in their lives.

Do you know what you really want in life? Can you get a clear picture of it in your mind? Are you willing to make some sacrifices to achieve your dreams? If you can answer yes to those questions, you are on your way to becoming more successful. However, to ensure that your goals are not just dreams, see if they pass the SAM test.

The SAM Test

The SAM test says that all goals must be *specific, achievable*, and *measurable*. I have found that if these three characteristics are manifest in your goal-executing strategy, you can accomplish what you desire.

Let's examine these three characteristics. *Specific* means well defined or limited to a certain kind or type. I believe that for your goals to qualify as specific, you must put them in written form. No matter how good your memory is, it is better to have your goals in writing. Examples of specific goals could include "I will lose ten pounds by April 1, 1996" and "I will earn $1 million by Friday."

While both of these examples are specific, only one of them meets the second part of the SAM test, which stands for *achievable*. It is reasonable to believe that I could lose ten pounds in three months. This is certainly achievable. It is not reasonable to believe that I can earn $1 million in less than one week. In this case, the dream is not impossible, but the odds are against it. That does not mean that you shouldn't think big. Goals should make us stretch and reach. Goals should make us venture out of our comfort zones.

The third part of the SAM test is that all goals must be *measurable*. If, for example, I had said, "I want to lose some weight," how would we measure *some*? How much is some weight? Some is neither specific nor measurable. Losing ten pounds by April 1 is a goal that meets all SAM criteria. It is specific, achievable, and measurable.

Get Plugged In

You can plug into the power of goal setting by following this simple process. First, set some realistic, achievable goals. Write them down, and break them into measurable steps.

Second, concentrate on the benefits of reaching those goals. Promise yourself a special treat or reward when you hit your targets.

Third, continually rub elbows with high achievers. Nothing will increase your ability to get motivated like associating with winners. Listen to them, and learn from them.

Fourth, keep believing in yourself. No matter how tough your present situation may be, you are still a worthwhile person who has something to contribute. Whether you're eight or eighty, keep believing in your potential.

Finally, take some time to organize your life. You might make that one of your first goals. Take each letter of the word goals and use them to make a final point: *Good Organization Always Leads to Success.*

Speak for Yourself

What terrifies nearly every American? Heights? The IRS? Snakes? AIDS? No, surprisingly, it's public speaking. Surveys show that speaking before groups brings anxiety to nearly nine out of ten Americans.

Speaking in public is, however, a key ingredient for business and personal success. Most business operations are series of presentations. We must communicate effectively to win and keep customers, to mollify creditors, to motivate employees, and to lead shareholders. The ability to think on your feet and communicate your ideas powerfully is a skill worth developing.

Harvey Mackay is CEO of the multimillion-dollar Mackay Envelope Corporation and the author of the best-seller *Shark Proof*. When asked about important entrepreneurial skills, he said, "Of the skills that they [entrepreneurs] have to have, there's no substitute for being able to get on your feet and make a five-minute speech."

Other successful entrepreneurs and business leaders echo Mackay's comments. Paul F. Oreffice, former CEO of Dow Chemical Company, cites three traits that he feels are essential for success. Number two on his list is the ability to communicate effectively. (Number one is the ability to get along with people. A fair question to consider is how you can expect to get along with folks if you can't communicate well.)

Other notables have joined Mackay and Oreffice in touting communication skills. The list includes former President Ronald Reagan, IBM's Buck Rogers, Malcolm Forbes, Mark Twain, King Solomon, and Sir Winston Churchill.

Three Common Elements

In the last four decades, I've had the pleasure of listening to many great speakers. I've enjoyed the remarks of corporate executives, political leaders, professional entertainers, and educators. Those who are most successful in winning the audience's approval have three common characteristics.

First, they possess unquestionable knowledge of the subject area on which they are speaking. You cannot explain to others what you do not understand yourself. The successful speaker either has knowledge gained through personal experience or has researched the subject thoroughly.

The second common element is sincerity. Good speakers earnestly express their convictions. You cannot convince others of what you do not believe yourself.

The third common trait is preparation. Successful speakers prepare thoroughly because they feel that being invited to speak is a privilege. Giving an outstanding presentation is the best way to say thank you for the privilege. Reading, rambling, and regular referrals to notes are clear signs of little or no preparation. Practice at home, not before your audience.

Building Your Skills

We learn to become better communicators exactly the same way we learn other skills. Golf is learned on the links, not in the classroom. Tennis is learned by playing the game. Most activities are learned and improved by practicing. Although you must have knowledge of the basic rules first, practice makes perfect.

One of the best ways to develop and practice speaking skills is by joining Toastmasters International. Toastmasters is a not-for-profit organization whose mission is to help people develop better communication and leadership abilities. Its program is designed to improve speaking, listening, and thinking skills.

Toastmasters' principles are taught in a nonthreatening environment. All members have the same goal—to improve—and so they assist one another in a supportive, positive manner. Even the shyest, most intimidated speaker will feel comfortable in the "we're all in this together" atmosphere.

The Toastmasters program is educationally sound. Con-cise, well-written manuals guide members systematically in writing, organizing, presenting, and evaluating speeches. Each member grows at his or her own pace. Millions have overcome their anxiety with Toastmasters' training.

As a professional speaker who makes most of my living delivering workshops, seminars, and keynote speeches, I value the training I received in Toastmasters. I still get ner-vous before every speech. However, now I know how to make the fear I feel work for me. I know how to turn the fear to energy.

If you would like to learn more about how to locate the Toastmasters Club nearest you, send a stamped, self-addressed envelope to Solid Gold - Speaking, P.O. Box 67, Amarillo, Texas 79105. Be sure to request "Toastmasters infor-mation."

The Law of Increasing Returns

We live in a land of laws. Laws are the foundation of our democracy. Laws protect us from others, and sometimes from ourselves. Men and women created most of these rules for liv-ing together. However, not all laws that affect our lives are man-made. Some laws are natural laws.

The law of gravity is one example of a natural law. If I stand behind you and throw a bucket of water up in the air right over your head, you will get wet. It doesn't matter if you know about the law of gravity or if you understand how gravity works; you still get wet.

The law of increasing returns is another natural law. You may never have heard of this law, but, like gravity, it still exists. This interesting natural law manifests itself in many areas of human endeavor.

Napoleon Hill wrote about this law in his book *Law of Success*. He wrote, "Render more service than that for which you are paid and you will soon be paid for more than you render. The law of `Increasing Returns' takes care of this."

I've seen this law manifest in small business, in the corporate workforce, and in my own life. I know it's true.

The Truth Hurts

Sometimes we do not wish to hear the truth. For example, a few years ago, Japanese officials suggested that American workers were a little on the lazy side. Labor unions, industrial workers, and many others rose up in protest. Not true, not true, they shouted. However, there is some truth in what the Japanese said.

When I worked in the corporate world, I had the opportunity to tour and work in some of the nation's largest industrial plants. I watched workers in steel mills, canneries, and automotive foundries. I observed thousands of American workers, and few of them do more work than that for which they are paid.

Maybe the reason they don't work more productively is that they don't understand the law of increasing returns. How often have you heard someone say, "That's not my job," or "I don't get paid to do that." It is obvious to me that those people don't understand how the law works.

I grew up on a farm, and I know that most farmers understand the law of increasing returns. They till the soil, plant the seed, cultivate the crop, pray for rain, and harvest in the fall. Before they get any return, they work hard and invest heavily.

If they plant one hundred acres, they can harvest no more than one hundred acres. Sometimes the harvest is dismal, but the farmers plant again. They know that they have to plant if they ever expect to harvest. They understand that the more acres they plant, the greater their potential harvest.

The parallel with business is interesting. We must prepare the business field, cultivate our customers, and provide valuable services. Only then can we harvest our profits.

Individual workers often find this process hard to understand. Most employees react to short-term incentives. The weekly or monthly paycheck is the most common. The harvest comes even if they loafed during the week.

Actually, the law is still in force, even though everyone appears to receive the same reward.When hard times come, management releases the least productive and least efficient workers. Therefore, if you are worth more than you are paid, you have additional job security.

In good times, the law of increasing returns improves your chances for raises, promotions, and additional benefits. Those businesses and individuals who render more service than that for which they get paid will soon get paid for more than they render. It's the law.

Networking

Whether you are looking for new customers, gathering business information, or trying to find a new job, networking is a strategy that can work for you. Networking is the art of making personal contacts that help you achieve your objectives.

One of the early lessons I learned in life is that who you know may be as important as what you know. I do not mean to infer that if you know the right person or persons, you can expect preferential treatment. Rather, I'm saying that you can enhance your success in life by building a network of contacts.

Business is all about building relationships. For entrepreneurs, this is especially good news. It means that you can enhance your business by expanding your network of people.

Frequently large companies lose sight of the basic principle that business is always people to people. Companies don't talk to one another, people do. Corporations don't make purchasing decisions, people do. Businesses don't provide outrageous customer service, people do.

The second part of this principle is that people do business with people they know, trust, and like. The ability to put yourself in a position to meet new people and then develop those relationships is a skill worth acquiring.

Making the most of your people-to-people contacts requires a little planning. Once you decide what events are most likely to bring you together with desired contacts, use the following tips to speed the process along.

Networking Tips

1. *Initiate the contact.* Put a smile on your face and extend your hand. Most people are just a little shy about making the first move. Your warm, friendly overtures will put them at ease.

2. *Gather information.* To determine whether a new contact can help you or you can help him or her, you must get to know more about the person. Ask polite, open-ended questions, and then listen.

3. *Arrive a little early.* Social hours are usually first, and are great networking times. If a meeting is worth attending, it's worth an early arrival.

4. *Develop a ten-second personal introduction.* This will help people remember you and what you do. An automobile mechanic friend of mine says that he specializes in hard-to-solve problems that other mechanics can't fix.

5. *Use your business cards.* Carry a good supply with you, and collect a card from every appropriate contact you make. When I attend long meetings, I frequently make notes on the back of cards to help me remember the contact. Notes about physical features, unique conversations, special needs, etc., help refresh my memory for follow-up networking.

6. *Give your full attention to one person at a time.* Politicians are notorious for looking past one person to see if someone more important has come in. Don't do that. It shows the insincerity of your intentions. If you find yourself in a dead-end conversation, wrap it up with a polite exit line like, "It was a pleasure meeting you. I hope to see you again at future meetings."

Don't Overdo It

A final point should be made regarding networking: Don't overdo it. If you spend too much time networking, you may not have time to do your work. It may also lead your contacts to blur in your mind, making it difficult to follow up effectively. You may not remember whom you've met, what you promised, or whether you followed through on previous contacts.

Depending on how busy you are, two or three events per month may be enough. If you make a few good contacts every month, you will have a strong networking base in a year.

When your network starts to work for you, remember your manners. Thank yous are always in fashion. A short phone call or brief note is welcome and appropriate.

Better Business Writing

A good business letter can win a new customer, line up a job interview, or make a friend for life. It can create a positive impression and make us appear competent, articulate, and professional.

On the other hand, bad business correspondence can blow a deal, destroy a good image, and cost us money. Why, then, are so many bad or mediocre business letters written? I believe there are three reasons:

1. We don't care.
2. We feel too busy to compose good letters.
3. We don't know the basics of effective written communication.

The majority of us probably fall into the last two categories. We care about our business image, but we are busy and we haven't developed good writing skills.

Because of our hectic pace, we need a simple method of learning and remembering the basics of effective business writing. With that thought in mind, I developed the WRITE method. WRITE is an acronym in which each letter serves to remind us of one of five elements of good business writing. These elements work with letters, faxes, and memos. However, I'll focus on writing letters to keep it simple.

The **W** reminds you to ask *why* you are writing the letter. Each piece of business correspondence should have a purpose and an objective. What do you want the letter to do? Thank a customer? Schedule an appointment? Resolve a problem? Inform the reader of your services or products? If your objective is unclear, the reader may discard the letter or delay action on it.

The **R** reminds you to get *right* to the point. Begin with the person's name and title, spelled correctly. Next, introduce the subject in the first paragraph. A good opening paragraph captures the reader's interest and shows why the letter is important.

The **I** in the WRITE method stands for *identify* key information. If the letter is referring to an order, use the invoice number and date. If you are writing a response, include the date of the original letter. If you mention a third party, give enough information to ensure that the reader will know to whom you refer. For example, write "Mr. William Jones of the ABC Company," instead of "Mr. Jones."

Letters that lack key information are a major cause of delays and the need for additional communication. When you give your readers all of the facts, it is easier for them to give you the desired results. Be sure to answer any questions that were raised in previous correspondence. Write clearly and simply to avoid confusion. Keep the reader in mind. A busy person wants to get the message in the first reading.

The **T** should remind you to write the way you *talk*. Use natural, everyday language. Typically, business letters take on a strange and cold formality. They are often filled with jargon and pompous phrases. Don't assume that using big words will make you sound more intelligent.

Each letter should communicate with the reader in simple, straightforward terms. With a little practice, you will be surprised at how simply you can state important points.

The E represents *editing* and *ending*. Edit letters carefully. Eliminate misspelled words, improper grammar, and excess verbiage. For example, "eliminate any and all words believed to be irrelevant or thought to be unnecessary" can be edited to "eliminate unnecessary words."

Devise a pleasant way to conclude your letters. If you are requesting an action, restate this in friendly terms in the closing paragraph. The reader should know exactly what you expect of him or her by the end of the letter.

Try the WRITE method on your next few business letters. You may find that you are writing less and enjoying it more. The real proof, however, will be in the results. You will accomplish your goals and experience fewer communication foulups.

Climbing the Ladder

One of my wise friends defines success as having as much money when you retire as your friends wish they had. He tells a little story about a farm implement dealer who retired with a million dollars in the bank. That, my friend said, was real success.

My friend went on to say that he asked that John Deere dealer to what factors he attributed his success. The retired dealer said it was due to thirty five years of hard work, paying strict attention to costs and expenditures, dealing with integrity, and the recent death of a great-uncle who left him $994,000.

That is a success story if I've ever heard one. However, most of us are not fortunate enough to have a rich relative who will leave us so well off.

I realize that some of you may not agree with my wise friend's definition of success. I'm not sure that I agree with a description of success that equates the worth of an individual with the size of his or her bank account. Personally, I've known some "no accounts" that had a lot of money.

However, I've never met anyone who would choose poverty and failure over success. Most folks I know would prefer wealth, success, and respect from their peers. Be that as it may, I'm certain we all have differences in how we define success.

Defining Success

Roy L. Smith said, "Success isn't measured by money earned but by service rendered." Elbert Hubbard wrote, "Some men succeed by what they know; some by what they do; and a few by what they are." Ben Sweetland said, "Success is a journey, not a destination."

Even wise philosophers have different definitions of success. However, we probably can agree on one point: We should not base our level of success solely on the end result. The true measure of our success should consider how much progress we make in our journey toward our destination.

Perhaps I can illustrate this point with an example or two. A physically disabled person who overcomes adversity to live a reasonably normal life and support a family may be a much greater success than a physically gifted athlete who earns millions from tennis shoe endorsements. The success of a poor person who, through hard work, rises from poverty to become completely self-sufficient may soar above that of the rich son who rises to the top of his father's company.

Success, considered in this light, is personal. It is a process of striving for what you really want to achieve. It is climbing the ladder to a point where you can thoroughly enjoy what you are doing and are compensated adequately for doing it.

Success is reaching a point of fulfillment in one's own life. Will Rogers said, "All there is to success is satisfaction."

One Rung at a Time

What about those of us who are not satisfied with our position in life? How do we climb the ladder of success? What can we do to attain respect, wealth, honor, fame, or whatever we feel would satisfy our innermost longings? How do we achieve the fulfillment of our dreams?

We climb the ladder of success one rung at a time. And, as the old English proverb says, "He who would climb the ladder must begin at the bottom." While this answer may appear simplistic, it is accurate.

You must anchor your "ladder of success" on a firm foundation if you aspire to reach great heights. The best foundation I can imagine is to have one foot of the ladder planted firmly on honesty and the other on action. Those who enjoy the fruit of their labors live their lives with integrity. They are also doers.

Alexander Pope said, "An honest man's the noblest work of God." Sam Houston said, "I would give no thought of what the world might say of me, if I could only transmit to posterity the reputation of an honest man." George Washington called honesty "the most enviable of all titles."

Success Factors

▪ *A sense of direction.* A common factor found in the lives of successful people is knowledge of where they want to go. For example, consider a factory worker who wants to become a foreman. The worker should learn about the requirements of the foreman's position. What special knowledge or expertise is required? Are there training programs, educational courses, or books that might help him prepare? The worker should direct his efforts toward that goal.

Consider the example of a small-business owner who wants to grow her business and hire additional employees. She might focus a portion of her time on developing a marketing plan to ensure growth, and also devote some effort to learning how to manage employees.

- *Not afraid to work hard.* Thomas Jefferson said, "I'm a great believer in luck, and I find the harder I work the more I have of it." I've known a good many successful men and women, and they all receive pleasure from working hard. I'm not sure whether their happiness comes from their hard work or from the actual work itself.

Study the lives of successful people like Henry Ford, Helen Keller, Norman Vincent Peale, Marie Curie, Billy Graham, George Washington, Wilma Rudolph, and Abraham Lincoln. You will find that not only did they love their work, they also loved to work. They were people of action.

- *Perseverance.* Another rung on the ladder of success is an unwavering commitment to do whatever it takes for as long as it takes. Edison might never have perfected the light bulb if he had given up after a hundred tries.

Here's another example: A young, aspiring artist submitted samples of his sketches to a prospective employer. He was encouraged to find another line of work. "You will never earn a living as a commercial artist," the employer stated. The young man didn't accept that advice. Instead, he practiced, studied drawing, and struggled onward. He developed his skills and eventually became successful. Today, Walt Disney's work is known around the world.

- *Enthusiasm.* Ralph Waldo Emerson said, "Nothing great was ever achieved without enthusiasm" W. Clement Stone calls enthusiasm, "the inspiration to action."

Those whose success we admire most are enthusiastic about their work, their dreams, and life itself. Everyone will love you if you maintain an enthusiastic attitude in everything you do.

- *Balance.* Successful people have balance in their lives. Although they may have developed one talent or skill above all others, they did not neglect other important aspects.

Some of the most successful people I know are balancing their career, family, physical, spiritual, and emotional needs effectively. By maintaining the balance, they enjoy happiness and fulfillment.

A final personal thought on success. I may never achieve wealth, fame, or other distinction in this life. Therefore, I approach every day as a short journey whose destination is satisfying in and of itself.

Chapter 10

Golden Advice

I've gotten lots of advice over my nearly fifty years of living. Some of this advice was bad, some of it was pretty good, and a little bit of it was brilliant.

In this chapter, I'd like to share some of the best with you. I'll start with three little lessons on how to overcome the dreaded career-killing disease called "it's-not-my-job-itis."

Then, I'll give you some advice on how to avoid growing poor by trying to get rich quick. (If you want to continue buying your weekly lottery ticket, it's all right with me. However, remember that you are gambling [spending], not investing.)

I'll also include some good advice for failures. I've had my share, but I've been blessed by being able to work my way back from them. You can, too.

In fact, if you examine the lives of most really successful people, you'll find that they worked their way back from failure at least once. They are not successful because they failed; they are successful rather, because they kept coming back.

Our lives are controlled not by our failures, but by what we learn from them. You can learn a lot from the mistakes of others. That's good advice.

It's Not My Job

We had been standing in line for several minutes. The restaurant was busy, and the order line was moving slowly. When we finally made it to the front of the line, we observed an interesting little scene.

The young person who was taking orders and running the cash register also had the responsibility for preparing each customer's drink. He needed to refill the ice container before he could complete our order.

This youngster turned to another employee who was watching and asked politely if the watcher would take the next customer's order while he went to replenish the ice supply. The watcher snapped, "That's not my job. I'm busy filling the trays."

The young man who was running the register apologized to us for making us wait for our drinks. Then he told the next family in line that he would return to take their order in a moment. He dashed after a bucket of ice, returned, and again apologized as he served our drinks. While all of this was going on, the watcher simply watched.

As we walked back to a table with our food, my wife smiled at me and said, "That was interesting." My daughter said, "Dad, there has to be a thought for your next book in there somewhere." I reached for my pen and a clean napkin and made a few notes.

The more I thought about that incident, the more I grew certain that I should write about it. I believe there is an epidemic of "it's-not-my-job-itis" sweeping our country. From our leaders in Washington through the young minimum-wage workers in business, this insidious disease is spreading.

It is easier to deny responsibility and just stand back and watch than to accept responsibility and get the job done. We need people in business, government, and education who can produce positive results. It doesn't matter whether we're serving our country or serving our customers, we must take responsibility for doing what needs to be done.

Three Little Lessons

Over the last few years, I've learned three lessons that relate perfectly to "it's-not-my-job-itis."

The first lesson is that folks who develop the habit of saying "I wasn't hired to do that," or "That's not my job," often find themselves without a job. An employee who tries to dictate to an employer what he or she will or won't do is asking for early, involuntary retirement.

This is particularly true if customers are involved. Specialization is a luxury many small businesses cannot afford. Therefore, we all must learn to do whatever it takes to keep customers happy—even if it's not in our job description. Don't forget that satisfied customers are our only long-term job security.

I learned the second lesson early in my own career. I discovered that if we look for work to do, we can always find it. When I earned my living on the farm, I found there were always fences to mend, equipment to repair, and chores to complete. In business, there are always customers to serve, floors to clean, windows to wash, and tasks to finish. The work is there if we look for it.

The third lesson is the most important one. It is this: If we want to get ahead in life, we often must put others' wishes ahead of our own. We must do what needs to be done, whether or not it's our job. Look for ways to make another's job easier. When you're dealing with customers, help them get exactly what they want, when they want it. We may find that not only is it our job, but it's also fun and rewarding.

The End of the Rainbow

I watched them stream out of the seminar by the scores. Their faces displayed a full range of emotions. Some were elated; they held the secrets of success in their hands. The wealth of the world would soon be theirs.

Others were disappointed; they had been believers right up until the very end. Wealth was within their grasp too, until the presenter announced the price of the miracle books and tapes at the end of the seminar. Alas, the $899 price was too high. They didn't have it and couldn't get it. The disappointment was plain on their faces.

Still others in the crowd remained unconvinced. They were skeptical of the claims of "instant riches," although they wanted to believe. In the end, their common sense prevailed. Perhaps a previous stinging allowed them to escape the salesperson's close unscathed.

Every day, millions of Americans are bombarded by get-rich-quick schemes. Seminars like the one I described are held all over the country. Thirty-minute television programs that are actually commercials disguised as talk shows fill the airways. Radio spots and print advertisements announce the "all you gotta do is" message.

Hundreds, perhaps thousands, are getting rich. Yes, it is true. People are making millions of dollars. Unfortunately, it is the sellers of these programs, not the buyers, who are accumulating wealth.

The Pot of Gold

There is a pot of gold for those who are willing to take from the poor so that they can be rich. They lure hundreds of thousands of honest, hardworking folks into these get-rich-quick traps every year. The sellers win; the buyers lose. At least, the buyers are the short-term losers in the money game. They give up hard-earned cash to buy a dream. They are searching for the pot of gold. They are short-term losers because they give up their money, not because they have compromised their character.

Those who use false promises to gain wealth are the long-term losers. Euripides in 413 B.C. said, "Wealth stays with us a little moment if at all; only our characters are steadfast, not our gold." A person's wealth is dispersed upon his or her death, but the character of the soul lives forever.

The Rainbow's End

The true end of the rainbow in this life is our character. What possessions we acquire are of little importance. What we own is no matter. What we are and what we become is critical.

Alexander Pope said, "We may see the small value God has for riches by the people he gives them to." I suspect Pope had his tongue firmly in his cheek when he made that statement. However, there is more than a grain of truth in it.

There are many unhappy rich people in the world today. Money brings only a temporary euphoria. We soon tire of possessions, and unhappiness returns. Riches and happiness seldom walk hand in hand.

Thomas Jefferson made the point well in a letter he wrote in 1753. Jefferson said, "It is neither wealth nor splendor, but tranquility and occupation, which give happiness."

A wise person once wrote that happiness is having something to do, someone to love, and something to look forward to. I thank God daily that I am fortunate enough to have all three.

My advice to each reader who would be rich is simply this: Concentrate on being a better person tomorrow than you were today. Work hard to gain knowledge, not wealth. Above all, ignore the get-rich-quick merchants and their messages. They cannot sell to you what they do not have themselves. Character and knowledge have great value, but no price.

Advice for Failures

She sat in my office close to tears. "I'm a failure," she said softly. "I really wanted this business to work. I wanted to prove to everyone that I could make it work. Now, for the rest of my life, I'll look back and know that I'm a failure."

There are times when I feel very inadequate as a business consultant. This was one of those times. I was sitting across the desk from a bright, young entrepreneur who was coming to grips with the fact that her business wasn't going to work.

The Lord did not bless me with divine inspiration at that point. Instead, I said something to the effect that having failed in a single business venture did not make one a failure, and that it was important to learn from that failure and go on. I reminded her that many successful people had experienced early failures before going on to great success.

I've thought a lot about that meeting and others like it over the past few months. You see, that meeting was not an isolated incident. I've tried to help hundreds of men and women recover from sinking business situations. Sometimes we're called on in time, but all too frequently we can only assist in cutting the losses.

I believe that experiencing failure in life is inevitable. If you earnestly aspire to achieve anything of value, you will experience some setbacks—temporary failures.

Therefore, I dedicate this book to all of you who have experienced failure in your life. Whatever you do, don't stop reading at this point. Please finish this thought. It might be your fresh start.

I can only guess at your failures. To list my own would take another book. However, it doesn't matter what our failures were—a business loss, a broken relationship, a lost job, or the resumption of a defeated habit—life goes on, and so must we. There is little to gain by looking back. Don't dwell on the past, and don't sink into the mire of constantly reliving last year's mistakes.

Don't Look Back

Satchel Paige, a professional baseball player, reportedly said, "Never look back, something might be gaining on you." As a young man, I ran track in high school. I learned that winning runners seldom looked back over their shoulders (you can see a lot from the back of the pack). Instead, they stayed focused on the finish line and gave their best to arrive there first. They did not dwell on past mistakes or failures.

The only great failure, the only true failure, the only lasting failure is *failing to try*. There is no dishonor in failure, only in failing to try again.

A Clean Slate

Every year life offers us a clean slate—a new beginning and another chance. We have an opportunity to learn from past errors and to apply what we've learned to new challenges this year.

Let's leave our failures behind us. Learn from them, yes. Live with them, no. Move on and look ahead. Today is the first day of the rest of our lives. Here's my wish for you as you read this book: May the happiest days of your life to this point be the saddest of your future.

Lowering the Standards

Recently, I read that a significant percentage of students who completed four years of high school could not pass the exit exams. Therefore, they could not graduate. After the announcement was made, a cry arose from the do-gooders. They claimed that the tests were unfair to the students who could not pass. Their solution: Lower the standards and let them graduate.

I began to think of what kind of world we would have if others picked up the philosophy of lowering the standards. For example, I considered the pole vault event in the Summer Olympics. Dozens tried, but only one cleared 21 feet. Unfair, the others claimed, so the judges awarded every participant a gold medal.

How would this work in business? Let's assume I got a small-business loan to start my business. I agreed to pay principal and interest each month. The business did poorly, and I stopped making payments. "Don't worry about paying me back," said the banker. "We'll just write the loan off.

Perhaps you hired a new truck driver. On the way out of your parking lot, the driver sideswiped seven cars. Then he cut the corner too sharply and dropped the trailer wheels off in a culvert. As the wrecker pulls the truck out of the ditch, you ask if your new employee has a driver's license. "Of course," is the reply. "I didn't pass the test, but I tried real hard, so they gave me a license anyway."

Constant Improvement

Stupid examples? Different situations? Not the same thing? Nonsense. America didn't get to be a great country by lowering the standards. We became a great nation because we constantly aimed at being better. It works in education and in business.

We are a world-class competitor in a global economy. However, if we begin to relax our standards for education, quality, or leadership, we will find ourselves in the morass of poverty-stricken third world countries. This is not the time to ease up or relax. Rather, it is a time to bear down, pull up, and set higher goals than ever before.

Now is the time to seek constant improvement. If test scores are falling, don't be too quick to blame the tests. If your business is failing, don't blame the customer or the competition.

Treat the Problem

Too often in this country, we spend all of our energy and resources in treating the symptoms, not the problems. Lowering educational standards to increase graduation rates does not solve the problem. It makes the problem worse.

Education is one of the cornerstones on which this country is built. Educated citizens build better businesses, are more productive workers, and are more capable of solving problems. We must have an educated workforce who can read, write, do basic math calculations, and operate computers.

If a large portion of high school students are unable to pass the exit tests, let us examine the cause. There are those who say that we don't spend enough money on education. From 1950 to 1989, spending on education increased by 370 percent in 1989 dollars. Test scores have declined since the early 1960s. It doesn't appear that spending more is the answer.

Was the material not covered in the curriculum? Was the curriculum not covered effectively by the teachers? Was there no support or motivation at home?

We may find that Johnny missed too many classes. Perhaps Johnny didn't study, or maybe he was too busy enjoying his puberty.

Our Constitution does not guarantee Johnny an equal education. It does promise equal access to the educational system, but Johnny has to do his part.

Let's be careful not to lower our standards and water down the value of a high school diploma. Mine still means that I can read and write.

Self-Fulfilling Promise

A woman named Mary had moved from the city to a small town. Mary hadn't found very much to her liking, and she was especially unimpressed with the service at a local store.

One day, while visiting with a new neighbor, Mary complained about the poor service at the store. She grumbled about the unfriendly attitude and how long it took to be waited on. She hoped the neighbor would pass the complaint along to the store owner.

A few days later, when Mary entered the store again, the owner greeted her with a big smile. He called her by name and told her how happy he was to see her again. He served her with gusto and filled her order in no time at all.

As he totaled her purchases, he expressed his pleasure that she had moved to the community. He was so pleasant and friendly that the difference in his attitude amazed Mary.

Later, as Mary visited with her neighbor, she reported the miraculous improvement. "Did you tell him what I said about his poor service?" she asked.

"Not exactly," replied the neighbor. "What I told him was that you found his store unique, thought his prices were wonderful, and had found him charming. I expect my dear, that the improvement came from his trying to live up to your expectations."

Psychology of Motivation

I don't know much about psychology, but I do know that we all prefer pleasure to pain. If Mary's friend had passed along her bitter complaints, I'm sure the store owner would have reacted negatively. Her complaints would have hurt, and the pain would have caused him to resent her presence in his store.

However, he believed that Mary found him charming, his store unique, and the service terrific. Her praise motivated him to live up to those high expectations. It became a self-fulfilling prophecy. The praise brought pleasure.

There is an interesting moral dilemma here. Mary's friend really didn't tell the truth. I am not advocating that anyone lie to make someone feel better. It would have been better if Mary's friend had tried to find something that Mary liked about the store and passed that along. If we look hard enough, we can always find something nice to say.

I remember a young lady whose mother had always told her to find something nice to say about everyone. Over and over, her mother had conditioned her to look for something to praise.

One evening at a dance she found herself paired with a very undesirable partner. He was homely, grossly over-weight, poorly dressed, and an awful dancer. All through their dance she tried to think of something nice to say. Finally, as the music was about to stop, she received inspiration. "You don't sweat much for a fat person," she said.

The Value of Praise

Mark Twain once said that he could live for two months on a good compliment. I understand exactly how he felt. Nothing makes writing easier than just one person's making a pleasant comment about something I've written recently.

Psychologist William James said that the deepest ingrained principle of human nature is the craving to be appreciated. We all need positive reinforcement to maintain a high level of motivation.

I wonder what might happen in the coming days if we all began to praise good work. How would our relationships with fellow workers, bosses, friends, and families improve if we accentuated the positive?

I challenge each of you this week to look for good work to praise. Be sincere, and make someone feel really appreciated. It may become a self-fulfilling prophecy.

Whipping Stress

On the way to work, you remember that the sales tax report is due today. Next, you recall that your fall inventory order must be in the mail by 5:00 P.M. As you sit down to get an early start on a full day's paperwork, the telephone rings.

An unhappy customer burns your ear for ten minutes about the poor treatment he received from your top employee.

You call that employee in, but before you can discuss the unhappy customer, the employee tells you that she is leaving and gives two weeks' notice. Then, the bank calls; it is holding one of your checks . . . . Welcome to the real world of stress.

The Stress Cycle

Stress is defined as physical, chemical, or emotional factors that cause bodily tension. Stress exists in varying levels in lives and, if ignored, can lead to dysfunction and disease. Many serious illnesses are linked to stress, and others are aggravated by constant high-level tension.

What can you do? Sign up for a stress avoidance class or attend a stress workshop. When you fully understand the stress cycle, you can more easily avoid lasting damage.

Much of the stress that we encounter comes from our working environment. Overdue reports, unhappy customers, undereager employees, and cash shortages may all be part of our day-to-day activities.

These environmental stressors lead to psychological stress where we let our feelings take over. We get angry, feel hurt and threatened, or perhaps become sad and depressed. We may remain calm on the outside, but inside we are churning and boiling.

Our bodies react to this psychological stress by increasing the heart and respiratory rates. Chemical and sugar levels in the blood system increase. These changes can lead to illness and lower productivity if the pattern is not arrested.

Just Say No!

Of course you should say no to drugs, but that is probably not your stressor. Learn to say no to unnecessary activities. Say no to nonessential meetings. Say no to too many clubs or service organizations. Say no to things that do not have to be done by you (delegate). Say no to busywork activities that do not help build your business or boost your career.

If you use nonprescription drugs (alcohol and tobacco included), many experts recommend eliminating them completely. Medical research indicates that the harm often outweighs any potential benefit.

One of the best hour stretchers and stress avoidance techniques is good organization. Walter P. Chrysler, who founded Chrysler Corporation, has been credited with a simple technique for prioritizing the work to be done. Every day, Chrysler made a list of the tasks to be accomplished. He moved the most important task to the top of the list and threw all of his energy into it. He stayed with that job until it was completed. Frequently, he found time to tackle most of the tasks on the list.

His secret, I believe, was taking the time to plan and organize. Only so many things are going to get done. Select a few critical projects and execute them effectively.

Exercise and Diet

Exercise may be one of the best stress relievers. Take a walk, ride a bicycle, or play racquetball. Transfer some of your aggression to the dandelions or your golf game. Exercise can help us deal with our lives in a logical and rational manner.

Dietary habits should also be modified to control sugar, carbohydrate, and calorie intake. Obesity not only causes physical stress on the body, but also tends to cause psychological problems.

A College Lesson

In 1988, I returned to college to finish my education. There are several lessons from those college days that have stayed with me. Perhaps none made a more lasting impression than this one from a speech class.

Mark Kissee and I were in that class together at Wayland Baptist University in Plainview, Texas. Mark gave a speech based on a ten-word poem that says: "Use it up, wear it out, make do, or do without." He had just returned from Africa, where he worked to support the efforts of missionaries. He used the poem to illustrate how missionaries handle the hardships that they encounter, and how they make so little go so far. Recently, as I reviewed my notes, it occurred to me that there might be a lesson here for all of us.

Use It Up, Wear It Out

A few months ago, I visited the offices of a very healthy, well-managed business. The owner has made a good deal of money over the years and is a very strong and generous community supporter. Because of his success, I expected to visit a new, modern, state-of-the-art office.

What I found was a clean, efficient, well-lighted older office with tile floors, sturdy but well-used furniture, and minimal frills. Except for the computer system, every major item in the office had been around for twenty years or more. The owner pointed out with pride that the business's original filing cabinets were still in service.

I have thought about this firm a number of times since my visit. The owner is using his assets very wisely. He is maximizing the return on his investment by "using it up and wearing it out."

There is significant waste in small business, in corporate America, and especially in government. What would America's financial condition be today if we had historically adopted a policy of "use it up and wear it out"?

Make Do, or Do Without

I have watched many entrepreneurs make do with what they have and can afford. It makes good business sense. Their businesses are healthier and more able to withstand downturns in the economy. They drive well-maintained older cars, look for bargains, and are not obsessed with the latest toys.

Making do with what you have is often a very good way to conserve capital for more important expenditures and necessary items. For example, most of the furniture in our office was purchased secondhand. We achieve a respectable and professional image at minimal cost.

Learning to do without is often an attribute of a very successful business. Long ago, I learned not to judge entrepreneurs' success by the cars they drive or the business images they project. Sometimes, new BMWs, high-rent office space, and state-of-the-art office furniture merely indicate tremendous debt leverage, not high profits and good management.

A good rule to follow: If an item doesn't produce profit, eliminate cost, or help you serve customers more effectively, do without it. I still survive without a car phone, a CD player, and a camcorder. My business car is eight years old and has nearly 200,000 miles on the odometer. This book is being written on a 286 computer, not a state-of-the-art Pentium-chip model. There are times when it is slightly inconvenient, but inconvenience should not be confused with need. Inconvenience is not a valid consideration in the cost justification process.

The "use it up, wear it out, make do, or do without" philosophy is also very good for our environment. It can be considered the highest form of recycling. Restoring your office furniture and driving the company car or truck another year conserve many natural resources, as well as business capital.

Some businesses may suffer as we move away from a throw-away business philosophy. However, when we consider the bigger picture of truly making the world a better place for all of its inhabitants, conservation makes sense.

Chapter 11

Golden ABCs and Other Gilded Thoughts

One of my earliest memories of learning is mastering the ABCs at age four or five. I can remember rattling them off for friends and relatives and generally being rewarded with a pat on the head or a, "My, what a smart little tyke!"

As with many other lessons in life, it took me a few more years to understand that learning the ABCs was only the beginning. To utilize the English language, in addition to the letters, there were phonics, words, sentences, paragraphs, definitions, grammar, and tense. The ABCs were only the beginning, a foundation to build on.

In this chapter, we begin with the ABCs of wisdom, and then go on to other valuable thoughts. You'll learn how good listening skills will help you be a better communicator, and how teamwork can build your career. You'll get tips on problem solving, and learn about a tranquilizer with no side effects. Finally, we share a few tips on how to negotiate like a pro.

The concepts in this chapter are as easy to master as the ABCs. Who knows, you may even earn a pat on the head. Now, there's a golden thought.

Words of Wisdom

The alphabet is a wonderful organizational tool. You can use it for filing systems, seating charts, and listing the names of several important people on one list without offending anyone. Kings and presidents use it, and it works well in phone books and dictionaries.

It seems only natural to use this system to organize my favorite quotes from successful people. So here they are: Words of wisdom in alphabetical order.

The First Half

- *Action.* "Thought is the blossom; language the bud; action the fruit behind it."—Ralph Waldo Emerson
- *Bible.* "A thorough knowledge of the Bible is worth more than a college education."—Theodore Roosevelt
- *College.* "When a subject becomes totally obsolete we make it a required course."—Peter Drucker
- *Democracy.* "Democracy is based on the conviction that man has the moral and intellectual capacity, as well as the inalienable right to govern himself with reason and justice."—Harry S. Truman
- *Experience.* "Experience enables you to recognize a mistake when you make it again."—Franklin P. Jones
- *Freedom.* "The natural progress of things is for liberty to yield and government to gain ground."—Thomas Jefferson (Natural, but not desirable.—D.T.)
- *Government.* "This country has come to feel the same when Congress is in session as when the baby gets hold of a hammer."—Will Rogers
- *Humor.* "A man isn't poor if he can still laugh."—Raymond Hitchcock
- *Intelligence.* "When you don't have an education, you've got to use your brains."—Anonymous

- *Justice.* "Justice is the insurance which we have on our lives and property. Obedience is the premium we pay for it."—William Penn

- *Kindness.* "A kind heart is a foundation of gladness, making everything in its vicinity freshen into smiles."—Washington Irving

- *Love.* "He that falls in love with himself will have no rivals."—Benjamin Franklin

- *Mother.* "All that I am, or hope to be, I owe to my angel mother."—Abraham Lincoln

The Last Half

- *Neighbors.* "The impersonal hand of government can never replace the helping hand of a neighbor."—Hubert H. Humphrey

- *Old Age.* "The problem with old age is that there isn't much future in it."—Anonymous

- *Patriotism.* "Abandon your animosities and make your sons Americans!"—Robert E. Lee

- *Quiet.* "The good and the wise lead quiet lives."—Euripides

- *Reading.* "Reading is to the mind what exercise is to the body."—Joseph Addison

- *Solitude.* "I live in that solitude which is painful in youth, but delicious in the years of maturity."—Albert Einstein

- *Trust.* "Put your trust in God, but keep your powder dry."—Oliver Cromwell

- *Unity.* "One country, one constitution, one destiny." —Daniel Webster

- *Vocation.* "Every calling is great when greatly pursued."—Oliver Wendell Holmes, Jr.

- *Work.* "Nothing is really work unless you would rather be doing something else."—James M. Barrie

- *Xylophone.* "I'm glad Webster spelled zilaphone with an x."—Don Taylor

- *Yesterday.* "I am not afraid of tomorrow, for I have seen yesterday and I love today."—William Allen White
- *Zeal.* "Experience shows that success is due less to ability than to zeal. The winner is he who gives himself to his work, body and soul."—Charles Buxton

Listen Here

A wise person once said that God gave us two ears and one mouth for a good reason. He intended us to listen twice as much as we talk. While this conclusion makes good sense, listening is not a skill that I have worked hard to develop. Some time ago, I took a short self-test to rate my own listening skills. I scored in the poor-listener category.

I know listening is important, so I decided to do a little research to see if I could learn to be a better listener. Maybe what I discovered will help you, too.

The Value of Listening

Many top executives rank communication as the most important factor in their success. Since listening is a principal element of communication, we can be more successful if we become better listeners.

At this point, we need to make certain that we understand the difference between hearing and listening. Hearing is physical; listening is mental. Assuming that we have no physical impairments, we hear 100 percent of the time. Unfortunately, we may listen only a small percentage of the time.

The value of listening is that we not only hear, but also can remember and process the information. This understanding allows us to become more effective with customers, coworkers, and supervisors.

Three Key Elements

The first key to becoming a better listener is to concentrate on what others are saying. We must focus on the message to ensure that we not only hear, but also understand.

For most of us, it is not possible to concentrate on two things at once. To listen effectively, stop talking, stop writing, and stop reading. Devote your full attention to the speaker. Make eye contact and send signals to let the speaker know you're listening.

Barbara Walters is one of the highest-paid interviewers on national television. She once described her interviewing technique to a reporter. She asks a question, then shuts her mouth and listens with her whole face. She concentrates all of her attention on the other person's answer.

The second key to effective listening is to listen selectively. Every day, hundreds of messages bombard our senses. Some of this information is not useful to us. Learn to tune out some of the messages and, on occasion, some of the messengers.

I once worked in an office where one of the employees obviously didn't have enough to do. This person carried on trivial conversations with anyone who would listen. Since I could not afford to waste that much time, I had to listen selectively. Sometimes I didn't listen at all.

I'm not implying that we shouldn't be sociable. Just recognize socializing as socializing, and don't confuse it with work.

The third key to becoming a better listener is to listen objectively. Everyone with whom we communicate has a bias or a reason to influence us. Therefore, we need to consider the speakers' reasons for expressing their viewpoints.

We should weigh each of our conversations mentally to determine the speaker's points of reference. What is in it for him? What axe does she have to grind?

For example, let's assume that I am considering a new car purchase. If I ask a salesperson, she might respond with an emphatic, "Yes, buy now." It would be to her benefit to sell me a new car. However, my auto mechanic might say no. He would prefer that I keep my old car, which may need frequent repair.

By understanding the perspective, I can objectively evaluate each response. This will help me make a better decision.

We can develop better communication skills. I encourage you to join me in becoming a better listener. By concentrating on the speaker and by listening selectively and objectively, we'll be on our way.

Geese Work

As a young man, I watched huge flocks of geese migrate north and south over the Missouri farm where I grew up. Over the years, I learned to love hearing the honking sounds and watching the big V formations fly overhead.

Although I loved the geese, I remember feeling sad as the flocks traveled southward in the fall because I knew that winter would soon arrive. Winter meant cold, bitter weather and more work to ensure the safety and health of our livestock.

The northbound flights of spring were early indicators that warm weather was on its way. It meant no more ice to chop or hay to feed. Spring brought new green growth, warm sunny days, and pleasant activities around the farm.

I didn't know about the wonderful lessons being taught in the sky as I performed my routine chores. I just enjoyed the sights and sounds.

Bill and Marty Geist, owners of Gingiss Formalwear Center in Amarillo, Texas, shared with me an essay titled "Lessons Learned from Geese." As I read the essay, I remembered those early farm days. I was also reminded that as owners and managers of small businesses we need to be alert for business-building lessons regardless of the source. I extracted several thoughts from the "Geese" essay. As you read them, I think you'll agree that we can even learn from the birds.

Lessons From Geese

According to the essay, as each goose flaps its wings, it creates an uplift for others behind it. Geese get 71 percent more flying range in a V formation than when flying alone.

The lesson we can glean from this information is that people who share a common sense of direction and purpose are more successful. They can work longer and accomplish more because they feed off the energy of others.

Another interesting fact is that when the lead goose tires, it rotates back into the formation and another bird takes over. This allows a fresh goose to keep up the pace while the leader takes a breather.

The message here is that shared leadership and independence give others a chance to lead as well as follow. While being the lead goose may improve the view, the work is harder. Everyone needs a break from the routine, and a fresh perspective may improve your attitude.

I also learned from the essay the reason geese honk as they fly. (It's not because they are passing another goose.) The geese in formation honk to encourage the leaders to keep up the speed.

The lesson here is to make certain our honks are encouraging. We all need a friendly honk from time to time. In business, it may be a word of praise or a pat on the back for a job well done. Encouragement is a good team builder.

The final point in the essay dealt with being supportive. When an ill or injured goose can't keep up with the flock, other geese will drop out of the formation and stay with it until it revives or dies. Then they catch up with the flock or join a new one. The point here is that your colleagues may need help from time to time. We should stand by them in bad times as well as good.

Teamwork

You've probably guessed by now that the secret of the geese's success is teamwork. The flock of geese really is no different from any business or organization. All groups can benefit from teamwork.

Teamwork is the willingness to work together toward a common vision or goal. Over the nearly thirty years of my working career, I've had the pleasure of working with some very talented teams. I've watched as the dynamics of teamwork allowed common people to obtain uncommon results. That is the value of teamwork: extraordinary results.

The word *team* even makes a good acronym: Together Everyone Accomplishes More. Together we can fly higher, travel farther, be more productive, and enjoy lifelong relationships.

I've also noticed that some teams dream of worthy accomplishments, whereas other teams stay awake and get the job done. What are the ingredients that makes teams successful? I believe there are five common factors you'll always find in winning flocks.

Five Success Factors

1. *Successful teams stay focused on a common vision or goal.* Every team member has a sense of the purpose or mission of the organization.

Successful teams focus on achievement. They focus on winning. They focus on execution—doing the job right the first time—and improvement.

If you wish to lead a successful team, make certain that every team member knows where the team is headed. Unlike geese, who intuitively fly in the right direction, your team members will have to be brought into the inner circle of knowledge. Let each person know his or her role and responsibility.

2. *All members make a commitment to the team.* Successful teams are made up of people who are committed enough to follow every task through to the end. They never lose their focus; they never let other team members down intentionally. On those rare occasions where a team member can't perform because of illness or injury, others step in to fill the gap.

3. *They look for ways to build one another up.* Just as the honking geese encourage the leader to keep up the pace, committed team members praise and encourage one another.

This may sound easy, but it isn't. There are times when we make more mistakes than progress. It is easy then to tear the system down. Winners are quick to praise and slow to criticize. Look for positive behavior and encourage it. Praise is a factor in strengthening every successful team.

4. *They have their pride.* Yes, I know the Bible says that pride goeth before a fall, but I'm not talking about a false, vain pride. The pride I'm talking about is the personal satisfaction that comes with the knowledge that you've done the job well.

Every job is a self-portrait of the person who did the work. Autograph your work with quality and pride. Don't be vain or boastful. Give credit to other team members. Build them up, and they will carry you with them—with pride.

5. *They acknowledge a leader.* Someone has to be in charge. Some team member must have the ultimate responsibility for the actions of the team. Acknowledge your leaders and give them all the support they deserve.

Next fall, as you look up and see a big flock of Canada geese headed south for the winter, I hope you'll remember this story. Also, I hope you'll be reminded of the value of teamwork.

Problem Solving

After working into the early morning hours, Terry had nearly finished getting all of last quarter's records on the computer. Suddenly, the lights flickered and went out. In a few seconds, the electricity came back on and all of Terry's work was gone. Terry has a problem.

Pat has worked hard to keep the construction project on schedule, because there is a $1,000 per day penalty for not completing the job on time. Yesterday, the supplier of the last major piece of equipment for the job told Pat that there would be a thirty-day delay in shipping. A thirty-day delay means $30,000 in penalties. Pat estimated the profit from the job at $21,000. Pat has a problem.

The day before Billie planned to leave on vacation, the company's number one salesperson requested a private meeting. She announced that she had received a much better offer from Billie's toughest competitor. She did not want to negotiate. She had asked for the meeting to give Billie two weeks' notice. Billie has a problem.

If you spend any time in business, you will encounter problems. Problems are normal, and to protect your sanity, you must learn to deal with them effectively.

Problem solving is a skill you can develop. It is a valuable skill that is needed not only in business, but also in government, education, and other areas.

Step by Step

The best way to deal with any problem is to prevent it. In a step-by-step approach, step one is to anticipate and avoid problems.

In the opening example, Terry lost several precious hours of data entry because of an electrical failure. While you cannot anticipate when an electrical outage will occur, you know it can happen. If Terry had saved the data on the computer every twenty minutes or so, most of the loss would have been prevented. A twenty-minute data entry loss is not a major problem.

However, you cannot anticipate all problems. Some problems will sneak up on you. Problems are good at that. So, the second step in problem solving is to identify the problem and the cause(s).

A good order to follow is what, when, where, how, and why. What happened? What are the consequences? What should we do? When did it occur? Where did it happen? How did the problem occur? How was it discovered? Why did it happen? Why didn't we anticipate the problem?

Often we ask who instead of what, when, etc. While discovering who caused the problem may be important later, finding someone to blame will not resolve the situation.

The third step in problem solving is to list possible solutions. In this step of the process, we are simply looking for all the ways we could solve the problem. It is most important to generate a lot of ideas. Brainstorming may help. Surround yourself with good, clear heads and start generating ideas. Encourage new and unique ideas and write them down.

The next step is to home in on the best solution. Eliminate ideas that cost too much, consume too much time, or require too many people. Take the best two or three solutions and refine them for further evaluation. One solution will usually surface as the most practical.

The next step is to implement the solution. The best solution will not work without successful implementation. Put the solution steps in writing. What exactly needs to be done? When? Where? How will you carry out the work? Who will be responsible for seeing that it's done? Remember, it pays to be flexible. You can expect to make some minor revisions.

The final step is to determine whether your solution is producing the desired results. If not, look for ways to get back on track.

Value of Humor

I love being around funny people. Most of my really close friends have a good sense of humor and maybe even a silly streak. They enjoy a good laugh themselves and love to make others laugh.

Max Barnett is that kind of person. Max and I have been friends for a long time, and our wives say we bring out the worst in each other. Actually, we bring out the best—the best memories, the best recycled stories, and the best new jokes.

Our visits are always punctuated with laughter. We often end up with tears running down our faces from just being silly. One of my fondest memories is the summer Max and I painted barns in Iowa and Minnesota.

The painting was serious work. We used a boom truck to paint very tall barns. Swinging in the air fifty feet above a six-inch layer of used alfalfa was no joke, but we did have fun.

Max knows that the world loves to laugh. He is an artist when it comes to being funny. He is also a very successful businessman, and I learned a lot that summer about the practical value of humor.

Max taught me that humor can relieve tension and negate harsh feelings. It can soften a negative message and still allow you to get the point across. Perhaps most important, a good laugh will make you feel better.

Natural Medicine

According to Arnold Glasow, "Laughter is a tranquilizer with no side effects." This is both accurate and true. Laughter is a good medicine. The medical community has discovered that good, hearty laughter has definite healing properties. Laughter releases chemicals called endorphins into the bloodstream. This natural medicine eases pain, slows the heart rate, and helps muscles relax. Doesn't that sound like just what the doctor ordered?

Today's small-business environment is a stress-filled, dog-eat-dog climate. Eight million Americans have ulcers. More than thirty million have high blood pressure. One of every five men in the United States has a coronary attack before age sixty. Stress can cause or aggravate all of these illnesses. A good laugh can help relieve stress.

It seems to me that businesspeople look for things to worry about. The poet Robert Frost said that the reason worry kills more people than work is that more people worry than work. Frost is probably right. However, it may also be that we all spend too much time worrying and working and not enough time having fun.

Work Can Be Fun

Work can be fun. Work should be fun. My work is fun, although what I do is serious. Many of my workdays are spent helping troubled clients—businessmen and women who have serious problems. Unprofitable businesses, tax liens, foreclosure proceedings, and bankruptcy are all serious situations. I do not take my responsibility for advising those clients lightly.

However, I cannot allow those problems to become too personal. I must not take myself too seriously, either. I must take time to laugh and renew. I can provide effective business advice only when I'm relaxed and clear-headed.

Therefore, I look for the funny side of problems. I look for ways to deliver the message with a humorous illustration. If the problem is not life-threatening, there is probably something to laugh about. Sometimes, just being able to laugh about our problems makes them seem less traumatic.

I encourage you to start looking for ways to lighten up and enjoy your workday. Do something uncharacteristic. Do something silly. Take time to pass along a funny story or joke.

Release some endorphins. Share some sunshine with your coworkers. Relax and blow off some stress. To the best of my knowledge, no one ever died laughing. So, lighten up.

Negotiation Notes

Once upon a time, a large polar bear who was hungry came face to face with a man who was cold. The bear saw the man as a solution to his hunger problem. The man saw the bear as a fur coat to keep him warm. They went into a nearby cave to negotiate. When the negotiation was over, the man was inside a warm fur coat and the bear wasn't hungry anymore.

In a small business, just as in life, the negotiation process affects almost everything that happens. Our success in business situations, marital conflicts, and buying or selling agreements is based on our ability to negotiate for what we want.

However, most of us are reluctant negotiators. We may feel that we will hurt someone's feelings if we offer less than the stated price. Perhaps we aren't comfortable with the situation or with the people with whom we must negotiate. We may believe that we lack the knowledge or experience to be effective. Past failures may increase our reluctance to try again.

However, there are some easy, commonsense ways to improve your negotiating skills. With the following tips, even the most timid can negotiate like a pro (with a little practice, of course).

Knowledge Is Power

Today, we live in the information age. When you acquire information it becomes knowledge. In negotiating, knowledge is power. Therefore, if you want to become a powerful negotiator, you must gain knowledge.

Learn all you can about the people with whom you're dealing. Gather statistics for the companies involved. Learn about the competition. Know its strengths and weaknesses. This information can help you in many situations.

For example, let's assume you need to purchase a new automobile. If you are like many Americans, buying a new car stirs up mixed emotions. The thought of owning a new car excites you, but you dread the negotiating process.

You can take control of the situation by gathering information. Read road test and consumer reports about the models you are considering. Purchase one of the new car cost/value guides that lists dealer costs for cars and options. Your objective is to find out what the car costs the dealer, then pay as close to that price as possible.

Next, check a used-car guide (blue book) to determine the wholesale value of your trade-in, if applicable. Check auto loan terms and rates at local lenders. You may get better terms from a bank or credit union than through the dealer's finance company.

Armed with this knowledge, you have the power to negotiate a fair deal—fair to you and fair to the auto dealership. The dealer must have profit to stay in business, so don't expect to buy below his or her cost.

Aim High

Research shows that those who have higher expectations achieve better results in all types of negotiation. Those who ask for and expect more, get more.

Have you watched insurance and utility companies negotiate with the government for rate increases? They start by asking for an 18 percent increase and, after months of hearings, settle for a 12 percent hike. It is very likely that, when these skilled negotiators go to the table, 12 percent is their realistic goal.

The secret is to start high and expect more. You can always negotiate downward. Of course, your starting point must be realistic.

Controlling your emotions is another key point. Never allow your personal feelings to influence the negotiation. If it becomes obvious that you really need or want something, you lose negotiating power. Developing a poker face to hide your emotions will strengthen your position.

No one wins all the time, and the best negotiations are those where everyone wins. However, you can increase your success when you have knowledge, high expectations, and emotional control.

Chapter 12

Golden Days and Memories

Like most of you, I cherish certain memories. Family traditions, life-altering events, and holidays are all golden times for me.

For example, Christmas and Thanksgiving are always days of family thoughts. When I was a kid, the Fourth of July was one of my favorite days because of the fireworks. Now it is special because I fully understand the price and value of freedom.

In this chapter I share a little of my personal side. Frankly, I debated whether I should include this chapter in the book at all. However, the faithful readers of my syndicated newspaper column, *Minding Your Own Business*, often tell me that they really enjoy the personal stories I share in the column. So these memories of special days, people, and times made the final cut.

I hope the story of Unlucky Jimmy touches you as it does me. And I hope you enjoy reading about all the things I needed to know that I *didn't* learn in kindergarten.

Your journey through this book is nearly at its end. I hope you feel that it was a worthwhile investment of your money and time. My wish for you is that your lives will be more meaningful, your work more rewarding, and your future a lot more promising.

A Christmas Story

"Unlucky Jimmy" is a sad little story my mother often read to me when I was small. It's about a little boy named Jimmy whose family was very poor. His little sister was an invalid and spent most of her days in bed. Christmas held no hope or joy for either of the children.

As he trudged home from school each day, Jimmy would stop to look at the toys in the bright store windows. More than anything, he wanted a little red fire engine. Jimmy knew he would never be lucky enough to get one. Also, his only marble had rolled down a storm drain the previous week. He felt that he was the unluckiest boy alive. He even called himself Unlucky Jimmy.

Then, one night just before Christmas, Jimmy received an invitation to a Christmas party for the poor children in the neighborhood. A nice lady from a nearby church mission promised Jimmy a special gift. Jimmy grew excited as he drew near the mission. He couldn't believe his eyes when he saw the Christmas tree. It was covered with lights and surrounded by toys. Jimmy saw a bright red fire engine just like the one in the store window.

When it came time for each child to pick out a gift, Jimmy's heart nearly stopped. He was afraid that someone else would pick the fire engine. Fortunately, when his turn came, the little truck was still under the tree. As Jimmy reached for the engine, he thought of his frail little sister at home in bed. He stopped and turned to the mission lady. He asked softly if he might pick two gifts, one for himself and one for his sister at home. The lady shook her head sadly and told Jimmy that there were only enough presents for one per child.

Jimmy looked longingly at the little fire engine. Then he picked out the prettiest doll under the tree. It had blue eyes and curly blond hair just like his little sister. As he returned to his seat with the doll, the other children began to laugh and make fun of him. Unlucky Jimmy clutched the little doll and ran from the mission. He stopped crying by the time he reached home.

Jimmy began to feel better when he saw the look of surprise and delight on his sister's face. As she hugged the doll and cried with joy, Jimmy didn't feel so unlucky after all.

Later, as Jimmy sat by his little sister's bed, someone knocked on the door. When he opened it, the mission lady was there. She gave him the red fire engine and explained to Jimmy that the children were sorry they had laughed at him. They had not known about his sick little sister. After she told them why Jimmy had chosen the doll, the children had asked her to bring the fire engine to Jimmy.

The True Meaning

I often think of Jimmy at Christmastime, usually when I'm feeling selfish. Would you join me this Christmas season in beginning a "Jimmy" tradition? We can make the coming year a joyous occasion for all people by giving of ourselves.

Volunteer time to your favorite church or charity. Make or bake something for someone less fortunate. Take time to listen to someone who needs you. Let's make this year a year of giving.

Remember, the real reason we celebrate Christmas is Christ's birth. It is His life of giving, sharing, and caring that we should emulate.

The Law of Thanksgiving

If I had been in charge, I don't suppose I could have picked a better time for Thanksgiving than late November. Thanksgiving and autumn are a natural match.

Crops have been harvested, and summer's fruits are stored away for winter enjoyment. God has painted the landscape with vibrant colors, as if to give us one last burst of glory before winter's bleakness.

Christmas is still a month away, and the Halloween candy is all gone. The World Series is still a pleasant memory, and the Super Bowl is an anticipated delight. It is a time for hayrides, bonfires, hot dogs, marshmallows, and cuddling.

The mornings are nippy, but the sun warms the midday for football in the backyard and last-minute chores around the house. Severe winter weather is usually a few weeks away, and so are final exams. Yes, November is just the right time for Thanksgiving.

However, I want to go beyond a discussion of Thanksgiving Day and get into the true meaning of the word *thanksgiving*. You see, there is a law of thanksgiving that goes far beyond the day or the season. If you understand the law, you can lead a more exciting and rewarding life every day of the year.

Three Stages of Thanksgiving

The thanksgiving law has three stages. The first is a warm feeling of the heart. This stage of thanksgiving is a personal one. It is a feeling of contentment. With me, it is a feeling that comes from hard work and knowing that I accomplished something worthwhile this day. It is a sense that all is well between me and my maker.

I often experience this stage of thanksgiving when I'm with my family and friends. It occurs when we gather to eat or when we are relaxing and sharing memories.

The second stage of thanksgiving is the expression of thanks to others. Our expression may take the form of a card or letter. It may be a phone call, or perhaps it's a gentle squeeze of the hand.

I'm convinced that there is a shortage of this expression in our world today. Genuine thank-yous are rare. We are too busy or too self-centered to experience the fulfillment that comes from expressing our gratitude.

Moving to this stage of thanksgiving not only is personally rewarding but also helps others. Often my load is lightened, my attitude improved, or my heart lifted by someone's simple expression of thanks. Like sincere compliments, thank-yous are a balm to the soul.

The Ultimate Thanksgiving

We are blessed as Americans. This truly is a land of plenty. We are blessed with freedom and a high standard of living. And through our blessings we have the ability to experience the ultimate thanksgiving.

This final stage of thanksgiving is to give of yourself in return. To be thankful in your heart is pleasant. To express your thankfulness to others is important. To give of yourself is the ultimate form of thanks.

The Bible teaches that it is more blessed to give than to receive. It has taken a while for that message to sink into my consciousness. Like most people, my first impulse is to get, not to give.

However, in recent years I've observed that the happiest people are givers. They are the ones who give of themselves without thought of reward or payment. They may not possess material riches, but they have what money cannot buy. They have peace, contentment, and joy.

Like the pilgrims of old, the givers can celebrate their blessings with those around them. However, for the givers, it is not just a day or a season, it is a lifestyle. To those of you who have arrived at the final stage of thanksgiving, let me express, from those of us who are still on the journey, a heartfelt "thank you."

Freedom to Compete

In his book, *How to Win Friends and Influence People,* Dale Carnegie illustrated the value of competition with a story about Charles Schwab. Schwab was the first president of U.S. Steel and earned a million dollars a year in the 1920s.

Schwab had a mill manager who simply could not get his mill to make quota. The manager had coaxed, cussed, and threatened, but the crews just wouldn't produce.

One day, Schwab visited the mill to discuss the problem with the manager. Near the end of the day shift, Schwab asked for a piece of chalk and turned to the nearest worker. "How many heats did your shift make today?" Schwab asked. "Six," was the reply. Without a word, Schwab chalked a huge figure 6 on the floor and walked away.

When the night shift came in, they saw the 6 on the floor and asked what it meant. "The big boss was here today," the day shift answered. "He asked us how many heats we made, and he chalked it on the floor."

The next morning, Schwab walked through the mill again. The night shift had rubbed out the 6 and replaced it with an even larger 7. When the day shift reported for work a little later, they saw the big 7 on the floor. The day crew decided to show the night shift a thing or two. They pitched in with enthusiasm and, when they went home that afternoon, left behind an enormous, swaggering 10.

Within weeks, this mill that had been lagging way behind in production became one of the most productive in the company. How did it happen? Schwab explained it like this: "The way to get things done is to stimulate competition. I do not mean in a sordid, money-getting way, but in the desire to excel."

The Desire to Excel

Competition brings out the best in business, products, and people. Henry Ford II said, "Competition is the keen cutting edge of business, always shaving at costs."

Today, America enjoys one of the highest standards of living in the world. Even our poor are comparatively wealthy. One of the reasons we have achieved greatness is our desire to excel. To prove our worth, to express ourselves, to win at the game of life—that is our motivation. It is not the competition itself that drives us; it is the desire to excel and prove our importance.

I find it highly interesting that the American who taught the Japanese how to compete frequently damns competition. W. Edwards Deming, the American management guru, recently said in an interview with the *Wall Street Journal* that competition is bad. Deming stated that all Americans think about is competition.

I'm sorry, Mr. Deming, but I don't agree. Every day I work with businessmen and women who care about their customers and their employees. They are in competition, but they are not focused on the competition. They are focused on their desire to excel, improve, and be successful. And they are succeeding.

Celebrate the Freedom

This year, we will once again celebrate our independence. On the Fourth of July, let us pause and remember that part of our independence is the freedom to compete.

We have the freedom to compete for profit, customers, and our slice of the pie. We do not have to agree with one another to enjoy our freedom. Adlai Stevenson said, "Freedom rings where opinions clash." Former President Kennedy said, "The cost of freedom is always high, but Americans have always paid it." Albert Camus said, "Freedom is nothing else but a chance to be better."

I pray that America will continue to thrive through competition and the free-enterprise system. Celebrate your freedom this week. Let us come together to thank God for our country and for the right to excel and better ourselves.

The Value of Respect

Comedian Rodney Dangerfield doesn't get any respect. That fact puts Dangerfield right in the midst of a group made up of politicians, lawyers, used-car salesmen, and parents of teenage children.

To Dangerfield, not getting respect is the basis for setting up a joke. To the rest of us, lack of respect may not be so funny. Respect is something that most folks desire and work hard to achieve, but only a few meet the standard.

Respect, according to the dictionary, means "to consider worthy of high regard; esteem." To me, it means placing value on positive personal characteristics that would be profitable to society.

I know that this subject may appear a little more philosophical than the rest of this book, but please stay with me. There is a solid message here for businesses and individuals.

Who Do We Respect?

A Harris poll of more than 1,200 adults turned up some interesting answers to whom we respect. The poll asked respondents to rate the moral and ethical standards of people in various occupations.

Small-business owners ranked at the top of the survey, with a 64 percent positive rating. Members of the U.S. Congress ranked at the bottom, with only a 19 percent approval rate.

The survey showed that the people Americans respect and admire most are those who create jobs, deliver honest value, keep their promises, and contribute to society. Perhaps there is a message there for Congress and our president.

Although small businesses rated at the top of the survey, more than one out of three respondents thought there was room for improvement. Therefore, to gain respect and ensure repeat customers, every business must be consistent in delivering quality and service that exceeds customer expectations.

Respect, is one of those words that has many definitions, but is difficult for most of us to define. I believe we place less value on respect in today's society than we did when I was a teenager. Or perhaps the meaning of the word has changed. I hope the following true story will help you understand my personal definition of the word *respect.*

Respect by Example

Helen was only thirty-one when her husband died. He left her with a heavily mortgaged farm and two young sons to raise. The boys were only three and six years old. For their sake, Helen decided to try to hang on to the farm.

The hardships of the seventeen years that followed might make a book worth reading. It would be a book about overcoming fear—like the fear that came late at night when a car drove down the isolated dirt road that led to the farm. Was it someone lost, or was it someone with evil intent toward an attractive young widow living alone?

It would be a book about hard work and doing without. Helen could not afford even simple luxuries like indoor plumbing and bathroom facilities. She milked the cows by hand. All summer long she worked in the garden so that there would be food for the winter. The boys' clothes were hand-me-downs from older cousins.

Finally, it would be a book about courage, love, honesty, self-sacrifice, and leadership by example. Helen taught her boys to read, to work, to fear God, and to love their country. She showed them by example the importance of integrity, the meaning of honesty, and the value of respect.

I know Helen's story well. You see, I am the younger of her two little boys. I learned the meaning of respect by her example.

Thank you, Mother, for your example. Today, I am beginning to understand and appreciate the sacrifice you made for me. I love you.

A Lot of What I Know . . .

A few years ago, I read a book in which the author claimed that he had learned everything he needed to know in kindergarten. Since I missed out on kindergarten, I started to wonder just how I learned the things I know. As I pondered the question, I realized that a lot of what I know I learned from somebody else.

My formal education started with the first grade. However, by the time I entered school, I'd already learned a few of the basics. I had help in learning how to tie my shoes, the ABCs, and how to count to 100.

I also learned some things on my own—for example, the flame on a match is hot, don't touch an electric fence, and running barefoot has some disadvantages.

The Roots of Education

The experts tell us that education begins early and at home. Psychologists inform us that we learn most of what we'll ever know by age six. If that is true, I received much of my early education on the farm four miles southwest of Galt, Missouri.

My father died when I was three years old. There I was, a fat, poor, white farm boy with only my widowed mother to raise and teach me. Today, of course, I'd be known as a horizontally challenged, financially disadvantaged, noncolor, agri-American from a dysfunctional single-parent family. You never stop learning.

Early Lessons

▪ From my mother I learned the importance of love and honesty. The love she showed by example was unselfish and sacrificial. From her personal integrity I learned that there is no right way to do a wrong thing.

▪ From my first dog, Buster, I learned about loyalty. For eighteen years Buster was a faithful, willing-to-do-anything, willing-to-go-anywhere friend. I never heard a harsh bark from him. He appreciated any small service rendered, and was always grateful for any food item I shared with him.

▪ From my older brother, Jerrold (notice that he ranks right after my dog), I learned that might is not always right. However, that knowledge won't keep your nose from bleeding. I also learned that hard work, practiced diligently, will carry you above the circumstances of poverty.

- From Arnold Rosenboom, my junior boys' Sunday School teacher and later my business partner, I learned that when God is the first priority in your life, everything else works out fine. He also taught me that we are in control of our own attitudes. When the going got pretty tough in his personal life, he never lost his good attitude and sunny disposition.

- From Sue, my bride of twenty five years, I'm learning about abiding love and trust. I'm also learning that for any partnership to work, each partner must build the other up. In marriage this simply means staying focused on the positive. There is enough good in the worst of us to keep love in full bloom if we focus on it.

- From my uncle, Robert Wetter, I've learned the value of consistent living. Uncle "Ribs," as we've always called him, was the first to take me on a roller coaster and to a professional baseball game. Those are memorable thrills, but what I remember most is his example of solid, dependable, Christian living. He has always been a man you could count on.

- From my daughter, Christi, I'm learning the joy and pride of fatherhood, and I'm learning the art of parenting. I've still got a lot to learn.

Lessons From School

- From Mrs. Irvin, my first-grade teacher, I learned the value of rewarding outstanding performance. I can still remember that brightly colored pencil I received for completing a difficult assignment.

- From Mr. Layson, my fifth-grade instructor, I learned that discipline really does shape character. It also makes sitting uncomfortable.

- From Mrs. McCracken, my eighth-grade teacher, I learned that respect isn't generated by physical strength or size. Mrs. McCracken stood about four feet six inches tall and weighed in at ninety pounds when wet. She earned our respect because she was, pound for pound the best teacher in the state.

- From Mr. Trower, my high school vocational agriculture instructor, I learned the value of public speaking. The ability to stand before an audience and speak forcefully, fluently, and convincingly is a skill everyone should develop.

- From Mr. Porter, our school superintendent and my high school psychology teacher, I learned that it is always best to think before you speak. It is frequently better not to speak at all.

- From Dr. Sartain, my college algebra professor, I learned that $x + y - ab + r + 2 =$ something. However, unless I plan to teach algebra, knowing the answer probably isn't going to feed my family.

- From Dr. Owens, my college history professor, I discovered that history can be a hoot. I also learned that any subject presented well can be interesting.

- From Dr. Mayer, my college journalism professor, I learned that there is a right way to write. I don't always write correctly, but I know there is a right way.

Lessons From Bosses

- From Frank Smith, I learned that all bosses like "hustle."

- From Bill Foster, I discovered that if you want to keep good employees, you have to pay them what they're worth.

- From Dave Hannen, I learned the value of being worth more than you're being paid.

- From John Stensland, I got a basic education in selling. He taught me that knowing your product and knowing how it will benefit the customer is a good start on making the sale.

- From Max Barnett, I learned that work is never work if you're having fun. The trick is either to work around funny people or to make whatever you're doing fun.

- From Joe Rich, I learned that if you want to be successful in the manure business, you follow elephants. That is, think big!

- From Dr. Jerry Miller, I learned to check references that aren't listed on the résumé for any potential employee. In other words, do a little digging if you really want to find out about someone.

• From Dr. John Dittrich, I learned the value of empowering employees. Make certain they know what to do, give them total responsibility for getting it done, support them when they need it, and reward them for doing it well.

Thank you all for the lessons. I'm sure there were times when you didn't think I was listening, but I was. More important, I'm still learning.

Give Me Liberty

"I know not what course others may take, but as for me, give me liberty or give me death!"

Who can forget those words uttered by Patrick Henry, the bright young lawyer from Virginia, as he addressed his state convention in the late 1700s? For more than a decade, Patrick Henry spoke eloquently in the Virginia House of Burgesses, on liberty, freedom, and independence.

George Washington attended the session in 1765 and probably supported Henry's positions on the early resolutions. Thomas Jefferson was too young for politics at that time. However, he often stood in the doorway and listened as Henry addressed the House.

Our founders spent much of their time seeking the blessings of liberty and independence. Liberty is one of the "unalienable rights" spelled out in the second sentence of the Declaration of Independence. Liberty is set forth in the preamble of the United States Constitution as one of the reasons for its creation.

What is this liberty? For what did our founders fight? Is it still worth fighting for today?

The True Meaning of Liberty

George Bernard Shaw said, "Liberty means responsibility. That is why most men dread it." Montesquieu wrote that liberty is "the right to do what the laws permit."

To this writer, liberty means freedom. Freedom to choose, freedom to learn, freedom to speak, and freedom to act within the framework of the laws of this great nation. True liberty is simply freedom with responsibility.

I love to celebrate our liberty on Independence Day each year. I thank God for our liberty. I am grateful for our nation, our leaders, and our freedom. Liberty is worth the price all have paid to date. It is worth the price that all will pay in the future.

John F. Kennedy spoke of his commitment to liberty in his inaugural address in 1961. Kennedy said, "Let every nation know, whether it wishes us well or ill, that we shall pay any price, bear any burden, meet any hardship, support any friend, oppose any foe, in order to assure the survival and success of liberty." May it always be so.

One Nation Under God

John Adams said, "Our Constitution was made only for a moral and religious people. It is wholly inadequate to the government of any other." Daniel Webster said, "Liberty exists in proportion to wholesome restraint." James Madison said, "We have staked the future of all of our political institutions upon the capacity of each of us to govern ourselves according to the Ten Commandments of God."

Yet today, there are those who wish to take any reference to God out of public affairs. The Constitution, they claim, guarantees separation of church and state. It does not. Read the First Amendment. The words *separation, church,* and *state* are neither mentioned nor implied.

What early Americans fought for was the liberty to be one nation under God. John Quincy Adams pointed this out as he reflected on the battle with England for our liberty. Adams said, "The highest glory of the American revolution was this: it connected in one indissoluble bond, the principles of civil government with the principles of Christianity."

The riots in Los Angeles—the killing, burning, and looting—would never have occurred if those involved had accepted the responsibility that comes with freedom. Following the Ten Commandments would put an end to killing, stealing, coveting, and hating. The problem is not lack of liberty and freedom, but rather lack of responsibility to protect it.

I accept the responsibility. I will not start a riot over a beating, a basketball championship, or a canceled concert. I will work within the system to right injustices and preserve equal opportunities. So please, dear God, give me liberty.

Index